STAMFORD TENANTS

STAMFORD TENANTS

a history of Rock Terrace
and its occupants

JOHN DAFFURN

Eptex

First published in Great Britain by Eptex in 2020
Eptex
40, Queen Street, Stamford, PE9 1QS

A CIP catalogue record for this book is available
from the British Library

ISBN: 978 0 9931479 2 0

Typeset in Adobe Garamond Pro, Baskerville and Darwin
by Bookstyle

Printed in the UK by Cloc Ltd

Cover Art – from author's own collection
Cover Design by Bookstyle

For Maggie, Sophie, India, Toby, and Isabella
who, even when able, may never read this,
but at least it's a 'show and tell' about their grandfather.

CONTENTS

ACKNOWLEDGEMENTS

The premise for this book was the discovery of tenants living at Rock Terrace and this phase would not have been possible without the ability to digitally search the *Stamford Mercury* from 1830-1911 via *BritishNewspaperArchives.com*. I am also grateful for the support of the *Stamford Mercury* Archive, the Stamford Town Council Archive, and the Stamford Library all of whom helped with articles and directories between 1842 and 1941.

For information about the lives of the tenants, I searched *Ancestry.co.uk*, *Findmypast.com*, and *FamilySearch.com* each of which provides access to different information sources. In addition to these digital platforms, documentation was also sought from Stamford Library, Lincolnshire and Northamptonshire Archives, the British Library, the National Archives, and *Google* searches especially within 'books'. I wish to thank these institutions who have helped me on this journey.

For the life of Richard Newcomb and his buildings on Scotgate, I was heavily reliant on the literature (see Select Bibliography), but this was enhanced by information from the *Stamford Mercury* Archive, the Lincolnshire Archive, and searches within other newspapers. This additional information enabled me to develop my own impression of Newcomb's character, publish new information about his building projects, and correct previously published factual inaccuracies.

This book was also lifted by the generous, and at times totally unexpected, support of numerous individuals who, having been tracked down, provided me with images, permission to use images, and additional information. They are included in the image credits.

Specific thanks go to: Sarah Critchard at the *Stamford Mercury* archive; Lucy Glen for local photography; John Hopson at the Stamford Town Council archive; Martin Smith for information and access to his digital copies of old images; Helen Taylor, and Kay and Neil Bamford of Rock Terrace who provided information and access for images; Peter Wilmot of PW Architects, who drew up the floor plans of Rock Terrace; the owner of Rock House who allowed access to view and photograph some original features.

Finally, getting my words and pictures into their final form would not have been possible without the diligent and responsive help from Sara at Northern Editorial, and the skill and eye for detail of Charlotte at Bookstyle.

Image Credits

I would like to thank the following for kindly providing permission to publish their images. *Stamford Mercury* Archive **1, 5, 26, 59, 65, 66, 69, 92, 95**. British Association of Paper Historians **2**. Lucy Glen **3, 6, 10, 11, 12, 13, 70**. TheOldBuilding™ **8, 17, 28, 38, 42, 80**. John Trotter **9**. cc-by-sa/2.0 - © Alan Murray-Rust - geograph.org.uk/p/6410204 **18**. Peter Wilmot, of PW Architects **19, 20, 21**. Graham Wright **33**. Northamptonshire Archive J(D) 936 **34**. Northamptonshire Archive J(D) 1028 **35**. Martin Smith **37, 40, 44, 67**. Recorded in the Edinburgh Gazette, issue 7717, 5 February 1867 **43**. SP Lohia Collection **47**. Stamford Town Council **49, 55, 82**. Andrew Fairfax **50**. Lincolnshire Archives STP 227 **53**. Patrick Marks **61**. Anne Elliott, grand-daughter of Albert Bassindale **62**. From New York Library **63**. DCM Medals **64**. Igor Grochev/Shutterstock.com **71**. John Cunnington **74**. The National Archives: J 77/1318/270 **75**. Helena Cutforth **77, 78**. Chris and Victoria Chattam **83**. AircrewRemembered **85**. The National Archives: W 361/1499 **87**. Commonwealth War Graves Commission **88**. Lynette Silver **89**. Margot Jeffery, grand-daughter of Wilfred John Hubert Twilley **90, 91**. All other images/illustrations are from the author, or others who prefer not to be mentioned.

INTRODUCTION

The death of a Stamford mayor, following an accident whilst riding out with the Cottesmore Hunt, might seem an unlikely start to this introduction, but without this unfortunate event in 1840, Rock Terrace would never have been built. This terrace of ten houses sits within a grouping of properties built between 1839 and 1845 by Richard Newcomb, the proprietor of the *Lincoln, Rutland, and Stamford Mercury (Mercury)*. These Grade II listed stone buildings are all situated on Scotgate, a road leading north out of the ancient town of Stamford.

Stamford was at its zenith in the thirteenth century: one of England's largest towns, with a population of over five thousand, and wealth based upon wool and grain. Since then one might argue that the town has been in decline, yet paradoxically it is often described as the finest stone town in England, and, more recently, is consistently voted as one of the best places to live in the country.

In the fourteenth century, when Stamford's wool trade fell away and the plague took its toll, its population began to fall, eventually by fifty per cent, and did not return to its previous height until the beginning of nineteenth century. In the intervening years Stamford became synonymous with, and eventually in thrall to, one family: the Cecils.

Although William Cecil, the first Lord Burghley, is the most noted of the Cecils, his grandfather, David, was the first of the Stamford Cecil dynasty. Both David and his son Richard became members of Parliament for Stamford, held offices of court, and as a result of grants from Henry VIII and Edward VI amassed many manors in and around Stamford. In addition, in the early 1500s, Richard Cecil was able to purchase the manor of Burghley, and later, in 1528, land known as Little Burghley, which together became Burghley Park. These early grants and acquisitions were the basis of the Cecil's wealth and subsequent power, to which was added the manor of Stamford, granted to William Cecil by Elizabeth I, in 1561. After his father's death, William Cecil demolished Richard's house in Burghley Park and built the magnificent Elizabethan mansion, Burghley House, in its place.

By 1800, the successive Cecils had effectively controlled the town for over two hundred years, and it had become a prime example of a rotten borough. Its parliamentary seats were disproportionate to its electorate, and largely under the control of the Cecil family, who used intimidatory tactics to sway the voters. John Drakard, in his *History of Stamford*, published in 1822, pulled no punches and marked the first Lord Burghley as the originator of this control. He said that William Cecil had 'laid the cornerstone of that corruption which had paralysed the vital energies of the town of Stamford, and of that tyranny by which the rights of the inhabitants have been held in subjection to the domination of his family'. This position did not change until after the Reform Act of 1867, and the introduction of secret ballots in 1872. Until then, as a result of their aristocratic privilege and immense property ownership, power remained with the Cecil family.

Stamford's renaissance in the late 1700s and early 1800s was fuelled by the growth in the coaching industry, as the town was an important stopover on the London to York route, and an important hub feeding Lincoln and the Fens to the east, and Oakham to the west. However, the benefits of coaching to Stamford were to be short-lived due to the arrival of the railway.

The decline in Stamford's coaching trade was exacerbated by the failure of Brownlow Cecil, 2nd Marquess of Exeter, to embrace the idea of the Great Northern Railway being routed through the town. Stamford lost not only its coaching business, but also the future industrialisation that followed the railway. At the same time, as the major landowner in the area, Brownlow Cecil prevaricated on the approval of an enclosure act which would have enabled housing and industry to be developed outside of the town walls. It was not until the Stamford Enclosure Act of 1871 became effective in 1875 that the situation changed, but by then the damage had been done. The town had become overcrowded and insanitary, made worse by the surge in slum courts built to house the poorer families, and industry had been lost.

Whilst the political radical John Drakard had been a vocal opponent of the Cecil's domination in the early 1800s, Richard Newcomb, through the *Mercury*, had in the main supported the Tory Cecils. This changed in 1830 when Newcomb became a Liberal and was in a stronger position than Drakard to carry the fight to the Cecils: he was wealthy, his newspaper had a high circulation, he owned much property (some inherited from his father), and he held public offices on the Stamford council. In 1847, Newcomb persuaded a barrister, John Rolt, to stand for the Liberal cause against the two Cecil candidates in the general election that year. At the time, Newcomb was mayor of Stamford and therefore the returning officer for the election, which Rolt lost. Shortly after, Brownlow Cecil, the Lord Exeter, evicted some of his tenants who had voted for Rolt, and this precipitated a petition to Parliament to appoint a select committee to investigate this interference. The petition was organised by Newcomb and was carried in Parliament by one vote, but the subsequent committee did not uphold the charges against Lord Exeter. It would be another twenty-five years before Stamford was released from the yoke of the Cecils of Burghley House.

From 1830, Richard Newcomb continued to accumulate property, becoming the second largest landowner in Stamford, after the Cecils. Some of these properties, situated on the upper end of Scotgate, a poor neighbourhood with many inns, hovels and tenements, would become the sites for his development of the area. The end result undoubtedly enhanced that part of Scotgate, but the grouping of the properties that Newcomb built was not planned. In fact, none would have been built but for the bankruptcy of a linen draper and the death of the mayor mentioned earlier.

Stamford, with a 2,000-year-old history, became the UK's first conservation area in 1967. A few years later, the Royal Commission on the Historical Monuments of England catalogued the wealth of listed buildings and architectural structures in the town, which included Newcomb's Scotgate buildings. Although Stamford may have declined in importance since the thirteenth century much of its architectural heritage survives, juxtaposed with schools, coffee shops, hair salons and restaurants, to support its growing population of retirees and commuters. It is a difficult balance as congestion returns to the town at peak hours, heavy goods vehicles are banned from the town centre, and the pace of life means that many are oblivious to the history of the buildings that they pass each day.

One of the Rock Terrace houses was my home for over twenty years, and I became curious about those who had lived there before me. In searching for the owners and occupants I discovered that for over a hundred years, following the completion of the building, the freehold of all ten terraced houses remained in the hands of only two families: indeed, the last freehold was not sold until 1969. The majority of the tenants of all ten houses have now been identified, and previously unpublished information regarding Newcomb's Scotgate development has been uncovered.

Since 1842, when Richard Newcomb first let the terraced houses, many families have passed through, including some of Stamford's mayors, aldermen, and Justices of the Peace (JPs). For more than a century, the properties were occupied by tenants who provide an insight into life in Stamford during that period. They came from all strata of society, some were *Mercury* employees, others were previously known to the landlords, and many were respondents to advertisements placed by the letting agents.

Births, deaths and marriages featured regularly, and tenants came and went as their situations changed. Happiness and heartbreak moved from house to house, and as the years passed there was a transformation in the social mix of the occupants. Each tenant had their own story, some mundane, some of historical interest and some extraordinary. All of these tenants, together with the landlord families, played their part in the history of Rock Terrace from 1842 to 1941.

CHAPTER 1

Richard Newcomb

For a period in the first half of the nineteenth century, Richard Newcomb was probably the most influential man in Stamford, after Lord Exeter, with whom he clashed on a number of occasions. He had become a wealthy newspaper proprietor and major property owner, providing himself with a powerful platform from which to attack certain injustices. However, he also used his connections and power base to influence people for his own ends. Today, Richard Newcomb's name is mainly associated with the *Mercury* and the buildings he erected on Scotgate, but by the end of his life he had accumulated many properties and parcels of land, most of which remained together, with successive Newcomb heirs, until their auction in 1919.

Richard Newcomb's father, Richard Snr, had owned a printing business in Uppingham and in 1782 moved to Stamford to help Mary Nott, a widow with four children, run her bookshop at 61 High Street. A year later they married (Mary was thirty-three, and Richard Snr twenty-two), and they went on to have four children of their own. Richard Snr became involved with the local newspaper, the *Mercury*, as its printer, and quickly formed a partnership with its owner, Christopher Peat. This resulted in the *Mercury's* office being moved from Peat's Maiden Lane premises to Richard Snr's larger house on the High Street, where it remained until 1971. As the success of the *Mercury* grew, the partnership prospered, but a series of personal tragedies led to Peat's retirement in 1797, leaving Newcomb Sr as the sole proprietor. This signalled the beginning of almost 150 years of ownership of the *Mercury* by the extended Newcomb family (see Appendix 1), and provided the initial source of wealth, which Richard Newcomb would later use to his advantage.

Richard Newcomb was born in 1784, the first child of Richard Snr and Mary Nott. When he was fourteen, his astute father, with an eye on the future, apprenticed him to the *Bury Post*, where he would learn the nuts and bolts of the newspaper industry. On completion of his seven years at Bury St. Edmunds, Richard moved to London as a reporter: the final phase of his journalistic education. Whilst Richard had been away, his father's management of the newspaper had been successful and the *Mercury* had continued to grow in both circulation and influence. In addition, his father had become an alderman, a JP and, in 1806, mayor of Stamford.

After a short sojourn in the capital, and with his father's business interests and public service burgeoning, Richard returned to Stamford, and in January 1807 became joint proprietor of the *Mercury*, trading as Newcomb and Son. The day-to-day management of the newspaper was from then on under his control, and Richard continued to expand its readership.

1. Masthead, *Mercury* 2 January 1807

By 1820 the circulation of the *Mercury* was the highest of all weekly provincial newspapers in England, and, in that year, Richard took a lease on a paper mill in Wansford. This upward integration, to take control of the main feedstock for his newspaper, was typical of his commercial prowess. He had secured a quality paper supply (the mill was already supplying *The Times* in London) and excess paper could be supplied to third parties. Two years later, Richard purchased the mill outright, together with the mill house, which would become Stibbington House – Richard's country retreat.

2. Wansford paper mill and house
   (later Stibbington House, left)

Richard's paper manufacturing connections probably led him to marriage. Like his father, Richard married a widow, also with four children, which may have been an indication that they had both been wedded to the strictures of editing a newspaper and, in their younger days, had less time for a conventional courtship. Richard was forty when, in 1825, he married Anna Maria Sharp, the widow of Stephen Sharp, a papermaker from Romsey, who had died six years earlier. Together they had no issue, and there are indications that their relationship, over time, became difficult, with Richard consumed by his work, and Anna partial to a drink.

As the years passed Richard, initially a Tory, became, in 1830, a radical Liberal, and began to campaign on various issues including the condemnation of the annual

Stamford bull run, and the support of Liberal attempts to gain a seat in Parliament against the might of the Cecil family. Richard's father died in 1834, and, free from his shadow, he pushed on with plans to make his own mark on the town. Three years later he purchased a one-third turn of the advowson of St John's Church for £120, apparently outbidding Lord Exeter in the tender process. It is not known if this was part of his regular battle with the Cecil family or a religious gesture, but years later Newcomb was highly critical of the Church and moved towards non-conformism.

By 1838 he had become a town burgess, a member of the Watch Committee, an alderman, and was chairman of the Trustees of Stamford Charities, taking on positions of public service, as had his father. During that year, at the age of fifty-four, Richard contemplated retirement and found a possible successor to edit the *Mercury*. Thomas Cooper, based in Lincoln, was a regular salaried contributor to the *Mercury* and, in September 1838, Richard told Thomas that he had bought Rock Cottage, on Scotgate, and planned to retire. In fact, Richard did not buy the house until a month later, at a bankrupt's auction, but must have been determined to be the successful bidder when he met Thomas.

Richard offered Thomas the chance to take over the management of the *Mercury*, together with Richard's dwelling above the *Mercury* office. Thomas accepted and, together with his wife, immediately moved to Stamford. But the excitement of such an opportunity soon turned sour. Richard did not move out of his High Street accommodation, instead giving Thomas only a couple of rooms in his house. More importantly, Richard could not bear to relinquish the management of the *Mercury*, nor retire. Poor Thomas was forced to resign, moving to London in June 1839, where he went on to become a leading Chartist, as well as a poet and novelist. The episode with Cooper points to the drive and passion that Richard had for his craft, and the purchase of Rock Cottage points to an element of luck associated with his future development of Scotgate.

Richard Newcomb had inherited property from his father, and also bought houses and land in and around Stamford, becoming the town's second largest landowner after the Cecils. Others have opined about the reasons for this accumulation of property, but when one considers the types of property bought, the circumstances of the purchases, and the development or planned development of the sites acquired, two probable motives emerge.

The first was his pursuit of a sound investment. Richard's initial wealth came from the *Mercury*, which he used to buy property. However, as a businessman with a strong commercial acumen, it seems inconceivable that he would be driven to purchase property for sentimental reasons, or to provide homes for potential Liberal voters. Instead, he must have wanted to continue to grow his portfolio and wealth, using the income generated from his property and the newspaper.

The second motive was to enhance his status and satisfy his ego. His vast property portfolio definitely strengthened his power and influence within the town during his lifetime, but he also wanted legacies which would endure beyond the grave. Certainly, his Scotgate developments qualified (see Chapter 2), and he also planned to build a new road to join St Mary's Street with the High Street, on land he had acquired from Browne's Hospital. The road would have been impressive, had it continued in the same style as the buildings either side of the proposed entrance on St Mary's Street. Unfortunately, these two shops with accommodation above, which replaced the George and Angel Inn, are all that Newcomb was able to complete before he died.

3. Shops replacing the George and Angel Inn

In 1847, Richard Newcomb became mayor of Stamford, and was the returning officer for the election in that year. It was a busy period for him as he was the main promoter of the Liberal candidate in the election, John Rolt, in addition to his civic duties and business interests. He had for some time also been training his stepson, Samuel Sharp, at the *Mercury*, in the hope that he might become his successor, although, unfortunately, Samuel showed little interest in assuming the responsibility of proprietorship.

Richard died, in his rooms above the High Street office of the *Mercury*, on Wednesday 26 March 1851, aged sixty-seven. He had spent the previous evening at his home on Scotgate, and, ever conscientious, returned to his workplace around midnight. His maid discovered him the following morning when Richard failed to ring for his post. He had been in the process of undressing and was found at the foot of his bed, his corpulent body having succumbed to a heart attack. He was buried on Monday 7 April, at Stibbington Church.

Without any heirs, and without an obvious candidate to manage the *Mercury*, Richard decided to bequeath the business of the newspaper, and all of his other investments and property, to his nephew, Robert Nicholas Newcomb, a Stamford surgeon. It was known then that Newcomb had accumulated a large amount of property, but this fact probably diminished over time as the portfolio was passed on to future heirs along with the *Mercury*. It may therefore have come as a surprise to Stamfordians when the extent of the remaining property was published in the 1919 auction sale catalogue (see page 104).

Richard's project to build a new road through from St Mary's Street to the High Street had floundered even before his death, but in his will Richard planned one last, and more altruistic, legacy. He bequeathed funds and land, with instructions to build a new school without 'priestly or sectarian bias', and outside the control of the Cecil family. Unfortunately, the Newcomb family were against this bequest and convinced the executors to abandon the idea. The school was never built, although years later the land was used by Richard's heirs to build Cornstall Buildings (see page 64) in St Leonard's Street, which over time housed a number of *Mercury* employees. Richard's wife, Anna, was not mentioned in his will, but later his executors provided her with an annuity of £350.

A few years after Richard's death, St John's Church underwent a significant restoration, and his nephew Robert funded, at a cost of £300, the replacement of the west wall window with a new stained-glass memorial to his uncle. The window depicts the Resurrection, and the bottom right-hand corner contains the shield of Newcomb's coat of arms. The shield is the same as that of Hugh le Newcomen of Saltfleetby, Lincolnshire, who travelled with Richard I to the Holy Land as a Crusader, and Richard would surely have approved of this posthumous legacy.

Coats of arms are not for use by anyone with the same surname, but rather by a direct male descendant of the original person granted the arms. It is not known if Richard was a direct descendant of Hugh, but in 1842, when he built his new home on Scotgate, he included, on the marble hall fire surround, the sculpted shield, in relief.

4. Newcomb shield of arms

CHAPTER 2

Newcomb's Scotgate Development

In 1843, when stagecoaches trundled down the Great North Road from York, their passengers' first impression of Stamford would have been a cluster of recently built stone houses. The Clock House, Rock Terrace, and Rock House were all built between 1839 and 1842 by Richard Newcomb, the wealthy proprietor of the *Mercury*. Even now, over 175 years later, these imposing Grade II listed buildings, having stood the test of time, still greet visitors driving into Stamford.

Previous writers have suggested that this development was either Newcomb's, partly altruistic, attempt to improve the upper end of the less-than-salubrious Scotgate, or was a defiant gesture towards the Cecils. However, recent research for this book paints a different picture. It would seem that this whole area would not have been transformed but for a large dose of serendipity, together with Newcomb's business instinct, and his ambition to be a powerful man of property. There was certainly no grand plan to conceive this grouping of houses, and research shows that Newcomb had to move quickly and audaciously, between 1838 and 1840, to achieve the end result.

Richard Newcomb had been acquiring property in Stamford, and beyond, since the 1820s, including some of the finest houses in Stamford, as well as plots with future development potential. By 1837, he owned a number of sites on Scotgate, including the Mason's Arms (26 Scotgate), which would later become Rolt's Arms. It is apparent from his development of Scotgate that Newcomb also acquired, during the 1830s, the Green Man Inn, with its brewery, garden, and stable block for fifty horses, and a property adjacent to the Green Man (see Appendix 2). Richard had no idea, at that time, how important these investments would become.

Richard's first move to build on Scotgate came in October 1838, when Rock Cottage suddenly appeared on the market. This large property had been owned by John Drakard, a competitor newspaper proprietor who, upon his retirement in 1835, sold the property. Richard Newcomb did not buy it in 1835; it may have been too expensive, or he may not have wished to purchase from an old adversary, whom he had previously sued for libel. Rock Cottage was instead bought from Drakard by a local linen draper, Robert Nickolls, who unfortunately was declared bankrupt three years later (Lot 2). Newcomb may also have bought Nickoll's draper's shop (Lot 1), which in all probability was 11-12 St Mary's Street (now Sinclair's). The advertisement infers that a draper's business had operated there from at least the 1780s, and it was still a drapers when the Newcomb heirs sold the property in 1919.

Rock Cottage was situated on a large two-and-a-half-acre plot that had previously been a quarry and, although not mentioned in the auction advertisement, it came with a small parcel of land on the opposite side of the road. Richard purchased the lot, possibly unaware of the additional land, and immediately made the best of it, kicking off his development on Scotgate. The triangle of land in question is situated at the junction of Empingham Road and the Great North Road, and had been enclosed as part of the Rock Cottage estate for over thirty years. Richard immediately razed the site, and built a small house that would eventually contain an ornamental clock, set into the front gable, facing down Scotgate, towards the centre of Stamford.

By the middle of 1839, when three-quarters built, the house came to the attention of Brownlow Cecil, 2nd Marquess of Exeter, who believed the freehold to be his. He sued Richard for trespass but, with likely failure, the case was withdrawn and Richard completed the Clock House (see profile 1) before the end of that year. The Marquess returned to the courts in March 1840, anxious to settle the ownership issue, and, although evidence indicated that his agents had not been diligent in the previous thirty years, his claim was successful. The judge ruled that the freehold did in fact belong to the Marquess, but only awarded him nominal damages of one shilling, and granted Newcomb a thirty-year lease for the land at a peppercorn rent.

Very valuable Freehold ESTATES, in STAMFORD.
To be SOLD by AUCTION, by Mr. JAS. RICHARDSON, At the Crown Inn, Stamford, in the county of Lincoln, on Monday the 22d day of October instant, at 6 o'clock in the Evening, subject to such conditions of sale as will be then and there produced, by order of the Assignee of Mr. ROBERT NICKOLLS, a Bankrupt, in the following lots, or in such other lots as may be agreed upon at the time of sale,

Lot 1. ALL those Two capital well-built MESSUAGES or Dwelling-houses, with large and extensive Shops, Warehouses, Counting-houses, and Premises thereto belonging, most eligibly situate in *St. Mary's street*, in STAMFORD aforesaid, together also with the Yards and Gardens to the same adjoining, as the same were late in the occupation of Messrs. Nickolls and Odlin, and now of Messrs. Nickolls and Groves, and in which a most extensive Linen and Woollen Drapery Business has been carried on for upwards of 50 years.

Lot 2. All that capital Messuage or Dwelling-house, called *Rock Cottage*, containing dining, drawing, and breakfast-rooms, 7 bed-rooms, dressing-rooms, and attics, with 4-stalled Stable, Hay Lofts, Granaries, Coach-house, large Garden and Paddock, containing 2 Acres and a Half of Land or thereabouts, thereto adjoining and belonging, together also with the Weighing Machine and Machine-house thereto adjoining, situate and being in *Scotgate*, in Stamford aforesaid, as the same are now in the tenure or occupation of the said Robert Nickolls.

All the above premises are Freehold, and in complete repair.—Lot 1 comprises premises calculated for a large and extensive trade, and lot 2 is fit for the immediate reception of a most respectable family.

Immediate possession may be had ; and two-thirds of the purchase-money of each lot may remain upon security thereof, if required by the purchaser.

For leave to inspect the premises, and for further particulars, apply to Francis Butt, Esq., Stamford, or at our office.   THOMPSON and SON.
Stamford, Oct. 4th, 1838.

5. Adv. for Nickoll's auction, *Mercury* 19 October 1838

PROFILE 1

Newcomb's First Development on Scotgate

The Clock House   Built in 1839

The Clock House was built on a small triangular tongue of manorial waste at the junction with the Great North Road (now Casterton Road) and Empingham Road. In the eighteenth century, this plot had occasionally been used by local farmers to graze cattle and, as with much of Stamford's other waste ground, was owned by the Marquess of Exeter.

Around 1804, a man named Goodwin erected a wall around the plot and set up a stonemason's workshop. Building on wasteland outside of the town was not uncommon, and, when noticed, the agent for the manor or the town council would fine the occupier, which in turn would often be converted into a rent. This happened to Goodwin who was fined £2 and, up until his death in 1815, paid £2 per annum in rent to the Marquess.

Across the road from this waste was Rock Cottage, owned by Colonel Denshire. In 1815, the cottage was occupied by Denshire's younger brother, Major Denshire, who, being annoyed by the unsightly workshop, went to the Marquess of Exeter to ask permission to buy out Goodwin. This was agreed; Goodwin's widow received £20, and Denshire pulled down the buildings, planted trees and enclosed the land.

6. The Clock House

By 1825 Major Denshire had moved to London, and in April that year his brother sold Rock Cottage to John Drakard. After buying the house, Drakard never used, nor laid claim to, the parcel of land, which was repossessed by the Marquess in 1826. When Drakard put Rock Cottage up for sale, in 1836, the detailed, and apparently overblown, description of the property made no mention of the waste. The cottage was bought by Robert Nickolls, who took down a section of the wall to the land, which had been rebuilt by Lord Exeter in 1826, and inserted a door. When this was brought to the attention of the Marquess' land agent, Nickolls was told that he would be levied a fine, which he refused to pay. Before this issue was resolved, Nickolls was made bankrupt and, at the ensuing auction, Rock Cottage was snapped up by Richard Newcomb.

The auctioneer was James Richardson, who knew Newcomb personally, as he rented 13 Barn Hill from him, and whilst the waste was not included in the auction sale particulars, Richardson was very aware of it. After the sale he personally took Newcomb to Rock Cottage, and also walked him across the road to unlock the door to the wasteland. Newcomb, upon taking possession, immediately pulled down the wall, felled the trees, and started to build a house which would become known, initially, as Clock Cottage, and later as the Clock House. The house consisted of two living rooms and two bedrooms, each room measuring ten feet by fourteen feet, divided by a central staircase rising from the front entrance. At the rear of the house were two further rooms within a single-storey extension, providing kitchen, scullery and sleeping space for a maid-of-all-work. The privy would have been situated in the small rear courtyard and the only garden to speak of was a triangle of land at the front of the house. It was not a large or grand house by any means, but it was built as a decorative house with gothic features, making the most of the small plot.

One of the first residents was Robert Shaw, a yeoman farmer from Swineshead, Lincolnshire, who paid £15 per annum in rent and may have used it as a town house or retirement home. His daughter Mary Ann was married from the house in 1847. More recently, the Clock House has undergone a sympathetic restoration, after which it was sold, in 2019, for £477,000.

In February 1840, another serendipitous event occurred for Richard. Francis Butt, the mayor of Stamford, was hunting with the Cottesmore hounds when he suffered an apoplectic fit and fell from his horse. His health declined over the following weeks, and he died at home in Stamford on 19 February. Two years earlier, Francis had taken over a twenty-one-year lease from Browne's Hospital, a fifteenth century local charity, for land and buildings on Scotgate.

Richard Newcomb, who was a Stamford alderman under Butt's mayoralty, may have been aware of Butt's investment, and knew Butt's executors, who advertised the auction of the lease in the *Mercury* on 26 March 1840. Newcomb was well aware that the lease on this parcel of Scotgate land was worth more to him than anyone else, and made sure that he was the successful bidder. The assignment of the lease was confirmed in a licence from Browne's Hospital on 23 April 1840.

The plot, then occupied by the wheelwright Henry Hayes, was of great value to Richard because it was adjacent to the freehold land, near the Green Man, that he already owned. In addition, the plot had a water pump within its grounds, which was a precious commodity at that time. This last acquisition (see Appendix 2) provided an enlarged building plot which, in part, became the site for his second development: the ten houses of Rock Terrace (see Chapter 3). By building the terrace opposite his new home, Newcomb was able to remove the unsightly tenements, barns and pigsties, and replace them with a row of attractive town houses, which improved Rock Cottage's aspect, and also provided an income. But there was an issue, which Newcomb must have resolved in his favour.

The Browne's Hospital land was only leased, yet Newcomb's plan was to tear down the existing buildings and build anew, which would have required, at the very least, the tacit approval of the charity. Richard Newcomb was unable to immediately purchase the freehold of this land, as charity rules prohibited the sale of trust assets. However, with Newcomb's knowledge of charity trust law (he was chairman of the Trustees of Stamford Charities), and his power and influence within the town, he must have reached an understanding with the warden of Browne's Hospital prior to building the terrace.

The solution was based on an Act of Parliament, passed around 1822, which allowed for the exchange, rather than sale, of charity assets, providing certain rules were observed and permissions obtained. In particular the Bishop of Lincoln's approval was required, based on the recommendation of a commission set up to establish that the proposed exchange was beneficial to the Browne's Hospital charity. The Bishop's approval was forthcoming, and in October 1842 consecutive advertisements were placed, over three weeks in the *Mercury*, stating that 'the Warden, Confrater and the Twelve Poor Persons of the William Browne Hospital agree to exchange land on Scotgate [Newcomb's leased land], and on St Mary's Street [the George and Angel Inn] for some of Newcomb's freehold land at Sutton St Edmund [about thirty miles east of Stamford]'.

The agreement was ratified in June 1843, providing Newcomb with the freehold, by which time Rock Terrace had already been built. Appended to a copy of the agreement to exchange land, in the Browne's Hospital archive, is a plot diagram of the Scotgate land in question. Interestingly, it shows the plot as it was prior to building Rock Terrace (see Appendix 2, image 93). Was it possible that the Bishop's commission were unaware of the profitable development of the site when they gave their approval?

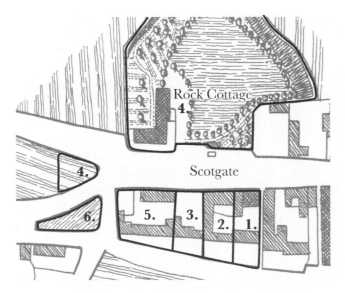

1. The Green Man Inn, 1833

2. The Green Man Stables, 1833

3. Property adjacent to the stables, ?

4. Rock Cottage bought in auction with small triangle of land opposite, 1838

5. Browne's Hospital land leased in 1840, freehold acquired in 1843

6. Small spinney, ?

7. Newcomb's acquisitions on Scotgate, on Martin Smith's drawing of Knipes 1833 survey map

The Clock House and Rock Terrace were built by Robert Woolston, a local man. After completing the terrace, Woolston's team moved across the road, demolished Rock Cottage and, in its place, built Rock House (see profile 2), a new town residence for Richard Newcomb, which became the largest property in Stamford.

PROFILE 2

Richard Newcomb's Town House

Rock House   Built 1842

Once Richard Newcomb had completed the Clock House and Rock Terrace, he was able to direct his team of builders to set about creating his own magnificent residence. The same architect that had designed the terrace was used, and the first step was to demolish the eighteenth-century cottage that Newcomb had bought in 1838. The new house was built on a large plot, which enabled Newcomb to set it back from the road, provide an in-and-out carriage drive with gates mounted between two stone piers, and surround it with a stone wall. Over time, trees would grow between the house and Scotgate providing additional privacy.

8. Rock House

The house consists of two storeys and a basement, with the main part built of ashlar and the rear wing of coursed rubble, with a Welsh slate hipped roof. The overall design, both exterior and interior, is classical with typical mid-Victorian embellishments. Externally at each corner sit giant pilasters, Corinthian at the front (similar to, but more ornate than, Rock Terrace) and Tuscan at the rear. On the roof, almost hidden from the road, sits a rectangular, glazed cupola providing natural light to the stairwell and hall below.

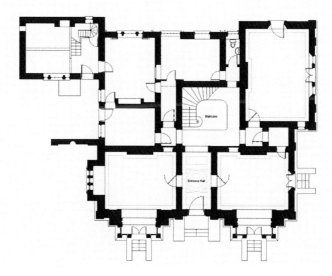

9. Ground floor plan

The ground floor layout, taken from a contemporary plan, shows the original structure of 1842 and little has changed since. Internally, the rooms, as one might expect for Newcomb's home, are more ornate than at Rock Terrace. Much use is made of decorative plaster ceilings and cornices, and the main staircase has a cast iron rather than wooden balustrade. In the hall, at the foot of the stairwell, there is a large ornate marble fireplace surround (believed to be original), containing Newcomb's shield of arms, inset with blue tiles (a later addition), and above, the glazing and ornate surround of the cupola.

Newcomb enjoyed his new home for less than ten years, dying in 1851, before the trees surrounding the house had matured. Following his death, Rock House continued, for some years, to be occupied by his relatives, especially his nephew and heir, Robert Nicholas. However, after the death of Robert in 1863, followed by his mother in 1866, the house became part of the Newcomb estate and was let to various families.

10. Hall ceiling   11. Hall fireplace   12. Shield of arms   13. Cupola

The size and grandeur of the house, together with its proximity to the centre of Stamford, and its large garden, meant that letting was not a problem, either to the gentry or the nouveau riche. One of the first tenants was Capt. the Hon. Charles Edward Hobart, son of the 6th Earl of Buckinghamshire and brother of Augustus Hobart, who was famously known as 'Hobart Pasha', from his time as head of the Turkish naval fleet. In 1871, Charles hosted the divorced Elizabeth, Princess of Schaumburg-Lippe, Baden Baden, for a three week stay at Rock House.

Other tenants included Joseph Boam, coal merchant, and Edward Blackstone, founder of Blackstone & Co who, in 1892, invented the first horse-powered mechanical swathe turner. Another was William Martin, founder of Martin's Cultivator Company, and inventor of the Martin Patent Motor Plough. Martin became mayor of Stamford for the first time in 1913 whilst living at Rock House, and was re-elected, and remained mayor, for seven terms throughout WWI.

In 1919, Rock House was auctioned along with the majority of the Newcomb estate property portfolio. William Martin successfully bid to buy the house for £3,000 and remained there until his death in 1928.

From 1928, Rock House has been used in a number of ways, most recently as offices. However, in 1944 it became the headquarters of the 1st Independent Polish Parachute Brigade, under the control of General Stanislaw Sosabowski. The brigade was in action as part of Operation Market Garden and fought at the Battle of Arnhem.

Interestingly, most of the original internal decorative plasterwork and other features remain intact, and currently there are plans to return this substantial property back to residential use.

Finally, and not mentioned in the triumvirate of properties above, Newcomb completed his development on Scotgate by building on the remaining land between the Green Man Inn and the newly built Rock Terrace. There in 1844/45, he built two shops (now 30 and 31 Scotgate) with a courtyard and a warehouse, together with a stable for Rock House at the rear. Above the arched warehouse and stable-block he also built four terraced cottages (now 12–15 Rock Road) with entrances onto the lane at the rear of Rock Terrace.

14. 30-31 Scotgate

15. 12-15 Rock Road

All of the properties built by Newcomb are clearly shown on the detailed 1:500 Ordnance Survey town plan of 1886, and remain the same on maps today, other than the garden of Rock House, which has been lost to a garage and a retirement home. The spinney that Newcomb somehow acquired has also remained intact as the subsequent owner ensured that it could never be built upon. The development of the upper end of Scotgate had certainly made an impact, and increased the standing of Richard Newcomb, but within a few years the fortunes of the builder Woolston and Newcomb's architect had waned.

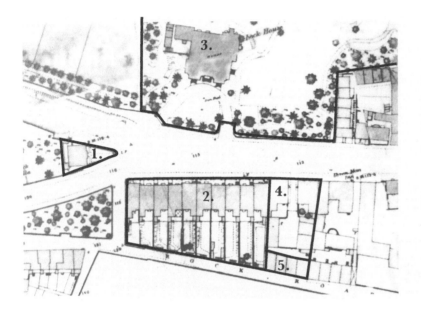

1. The Clock House, 1839

2. Rock Terrace, 1841

3. Rock House, 1842

4. 30-31 Scotgate, c1844 (with stable and warehouse)

5. 12-15 Rock Road, c1845 (built above stable and warehouse)

16. Newcomb's Scotgate developments

In recent times, details of the architect have been unknown. Pevsner in his *The Buildings of England: Lincolnshire*, published in 1968, describes Rock Terrace, as 'an ambitious row of 1841', and Rock House with an 'architect unknown'. In the more detailed *Inventory of the Historical Monuments in the Town of Stamford*, a survey published in 1977 by The Royal Commission on Historical Monuments of England, the architect for Rock House is also not mentioned. However, new research for this book has identified the architect for both Rock Terrace and Rock House as George Glover, of Pocock & Glover, Huntingdon. Also, whilst Robert Woolston was the lead builder, handling the masonry and plastering of these properties, the carpentry and plumbing was provided by Charles Collins, also from Stamford.

It seems that the relationship between Newcomb, his architect and his builders began in 1835, when St Michael's church was being rebuilt. The church, except for the eighteenth-century tower, had collapsed in 1832 after pillars were removed to make room for pews. Newcomb was on the building committee, which chose the plans of John Brown, an architect from Norwich, for the new church. Glover, a young architect, was clerk of works for the project, whilst Woolston and Collins carried out the work. By all accounts it was a successful build; John Brown was praised at the opening, and one assumes the others bathed in reflected glory. Later, George Glover made an impressive drawing of the north-east view of the church, which was inscribed 'to the Gentlemen of the Building Committee', and in 1838 it was reproduced by Day and Haghe, lithographers to the Queen. Newcomb must have been satisfied with this trio of Glover, Woolston and Collins as they became responsible for Rock Terrace and Rock House.

There is little archival information relating to Pocock & Glover although it is known that they were the architects for the Huntingdon Literary and Scientific Institution, which opened in 1842. It is now known as the Commemorative Hall. George Glover joined James William Pocock as a partner in May 1840 and assumed responsibility for Newcomb's Scotgate buildings, and during the build of Rock Terrace, in 1841, Glover married Pocock's daughter, Ann. Possibly on the back of the successful completion of the Scotgate buildings Pocock & Glover opened a representative office on Market Hill in Peterborough (now Cathedral Square), but a few years later Pocock & Glover became embroiled in a court case heard at Lincoln assizes.

Richard Newcomb, who had hired the team who built St Michael's, now fell out with them over money. He had withheld £1,406 of the building cost from Robert Woolston and Charles Collins, as he believed he had been overcharged, and inferred that there had been collusion between them and the architect. Collins and Woolston sued Newcomb for the outstanding amount, and the case was first heard in February 1845. Later that year the Pocock & Glover partnership was dissolved with each man continuing to trade on his own account. It is not known whether this was James Pocock distancing himself from his son-in-law or George Glover protecting his father-in-law from any potential fall-out from the court case. By March 1846 the case was still unsettled, although Newcomb had by then deposited £550 into the court, subject to its final decision, which the lawyers agreed should be settled by arbitration. The case was finally settled in favour of Woolston and Collins, who received a total of £1,070, which was still short of their total invoices. The proceedings and decision of Woolston v Newcomb at Lincoln assizes were never reported by the *Mercury*, probably censored by Newcomb, but the rival *Lincolnshire Chronicle* was happy to oblige, reporting that 'Considerable interest is excited in Stamford'.

In 1847, James Pocock died and George Glover was declared bankrupt, as he was 'embarrassed with railway speculation'. Robert Woolston's fate was similar to that of George, as having been awarded the contract to replace the Town Bridge, over the

River Welland, it made a loss, and, in 1848, he was also forced into bankruptcy. His nephew, John Woolston, continued the family business, and later became involved in the Rock Terrace drainage scheme. (see page 38)

CHAPTER 3

Rock Terrace

The completion of Rock Terrace, in 1841, transformed the upper end of Scotgate, replacing unsightly tenements and hovels with imposing residences. New homes of this size and style were rare at this time in Stamford due to the lack of space for development within the town. Nevertheless, despite the advantages of being new, having water supplied, having a garden, and being away from the stench and insanitary conditions within the town, these properties were not immediately snapped up. The rent of around £25 per annum, building work continuing opposite and adjacent to the terrace, and the dubious reputation of Scotgate, may all have contributed to this initial reticence.

17. Rock Terrace

Newcomb had built an architecturally uniform terrace, designed by George Glover, to rival the not so uniform Rutland Terrace built ten years previously. The two central houses (nos. 5 and 6) and the end houses (nos. 1 and 10) break forward with Corinthian pilasters at the corners, and the centre of the terrace is enhanced with a stone balcony containing the initials RN. Each house has a half-basement, ground floor and first floor, containing the bedrooms, with nos. 5 and 6 having a second floor, providing additional bedrooms. The internal floor plan was almost identical in each house, with the layout of nos. 1 to 5 mirroring those of 6 to 10. As there are no archived floor plans for the terrace, the examples below have been compiled from contemporary sources, using the layout that would have originally applied to nos. 2, 3 and 4 as an example. The highlighted rear extension, above the coal room, is explained later in this chapter. These plans provide an indication of the lifestyle of the initial Rock Terrace tenants.

18. RN initials at Rock Terrace

19. Basement   20. Ground floor   21. First floor

The engine room of each house was its half-basement, so called because the ceiling is above ground level, enabling windows to be included to provide light, both front and back. This was the domain of the maid-of-all-work, a servant, at least one of which was employed until 1900 in all of the Rock Terrace houses. Mary Ann Fryer started at 3 Rock Terrace in 1851 at the age of sixteen. She was the seventh of ten children of an agricultural labourer from Swaysfield, Lincolnshire, and had no alternative other than to join the legion of young girls in service, whose main hope of escaping that life was to marry.

The largest basement space was the kitchen at the front of the house, with light and ventilation provided by a large sash window looking up into the front garden. Set within the chimney breast would have been a black cast-iron kitchen range, and on the opposite wall doors led to the larder and the scullery. The kitchen would also have been Mary's sleeping quarters, and where she would rise each morning around six to light the range.

Daily life for Mary would have been long and harsh, firstly the living room grates would need to be cleared of ash, and coal taken from the coal room to reset the fires. Cleaning the dining room, and making and serving breakfast, would follow. After breakfast the dishes and pans would be washed in the scullery, and returned to the pantry, before Mary could move upstairs to empty chamber pots into a slop pail and make the beds. More cleaning would follow before preparing, cooking and serving the lunch and clearing away. In the afternoon, sewing, mending and boot cleaning might take place, out of sight in the kitchen, followed by the same rituals of setting the dining room, cooking, serving and clearing up for tea and dinner. The days would also be interspersed with specific weekly cleaning chores, including the black-leading of the range and cast-iron fireplaces, until finally Mary Ann, sometime after nine each night, was able to retire. On Sundays, attendance at church or chapel was usually allowed, and once every few weeks a Sunday afternoon off might be granted.

Mary would also have to receive deliveries and run errands. Provisions might be delivered in the morning, as was water, by the barrel, from the well situated in an underground room beneath the gardens of 6 and 7 Rock Terrace. Regular coal deliveries would come to the garden entrance and be dropped through a manhole into the coal room, next to the scullery. The dust would be a constant nuisance in the scullery, but at least the crockery and pans were protected within the enclosed pantry, which had a window to provide light during the day, via the scullery window opposite.

The relationship between the maid and her master or mistress would vary tremendously, as with all employer–employee relationships, but, in 1851, Mary Ann at least had the protection of the new Apprentices and Servants Act. This required employers of servants under the age of eighteen to provide adequate food, clothing and lodging, as well as an annual salary. Ten years later, Mary returned to Swaysfield to look after her parents, who were in their sixties, as her other siblings had left home. Mary never married, cared for her parents until they died, and in 1901, at the age of sixty-seven, was described as feeble-minded, although still capable of living on her own. In 1919 she died in Kesteven county asylum.

One of a maid's regular chores was to clean the hall – important, because it provided the first impression to a visitor or caller. At Rock Terrace, the hall flooring would have been boards, partially covered with a woven rug, leading under an internal arch supported by decorative corbels. Dado rails and deep skirting boards ran along either wall, and, beyond the arch, the staircase, with a plain, wooden, right-hand volute bannister rail and square spindles, was visible. The dog-leg hallway continued past the stairs, leading to the rear entrance and a door under the main staircase, which opened to steep and narrow steps to the basement: well-trodden daily by the maid.

22. Hall   23. Basement stairs

The ground floor contained two rooms: a dining room at the rear, which may have doubled as a day parlour, and a more formal drawing room at the front of the house. These rooms could be closed off by large, panelled, sliding, pocket doors – one of the features built by Newcomb's carpenter, Charles Collins. Some of these sliding doors are still intact in the terrace today. This floor was effectively the showpiece of the house, where the master or mistress would spend their days, and where visitors would be entertained. Other than serving meals, the maid would not expect to be seen in this area of the house whilst occupied by her employer's family.

The central features of the dining and drawing rooms were identical black cast-iron fireplaces, with a column of inset tiles on either side, and with a white marble mantle and surround. The marble surrounds were probably made by George Fearn, an acquaintance of Newcomb who had a workshop on the High Street, and who later moved into one of the shops Newcomb built, adjacent to 1 Rock Terrace. At least two of these 180-year-old fireplaces and surrounds have survived in the terrace.

24. Brass runner for sliding door

25. Drawing room fireplace

Whereas today fashion dictates light shades within a house, to reflect light and to create an illusion of space, the opposite was the case in a Victorian home, despite the absence of effective lighting. The floorboards in the drawing room would be covered with low pile rugs, possibly Kidderminster weave, and the walls would be papered in dark colours, and peppered with mirrors, prints, ornaments and knick-knacks. In addition, the furniture would almost entirely be made of mahogany (sofa, armchairs, card tables, etc.), as evidenced by the sale of household furniture by an unknown early tenant who moved out of no. 8 in 1846.

To the front of the drawing room, large glass, double doors opened onto a cast-iron balcony. These doors could be protected by folding wooden shutters, and were also covered with full-length heavy moreen curtains, possibly burgundy or dark green in colour. The sheer volume of individual pieces in the drawing room, many of which would have been draped with fabric, or bowed, provided a daunting task for the maid's weekly clean.

The dining room was slightly smaller than the drawing room, but contained similar large glass doors, overlooking the rear garden and opening to a cast-iron Juliet balcony – a protection against the drop to the basement level. Although all of the front balconies remain intact today, most, if not all, of the Juliet balconies no longer exist, as together with the front railings they were removed in 1944 for the war effort.

The first floor contained three bedrooms. The good-sized first bedroom, at the top of the stairs, had a window seat set into the thick rear wall, facing the garden, with a sash window above. The next, and

STAMFORD.——*Valuable HOUSEHOLD FURNITURE, CHINA, GLASS, and EFFECTS,* To be SOLD by AUCTION, By Messrs. RICHARDSON, On Wednesday the 21st day of January, 1846, upon the premises, No. 8, Rock-terrace, Scotgate;

COMPRISING handsome four-post, french, and half-tester bedsteads, with moreen and other hangings, wool and straw mattresses, excellent goose-coat feather beds and bedding, brussels, kidderminster, and stair carpets and hearth-rugs, 2 handsome mahogany loo tables, handsome mahogany sofa with carved front and back, mahogany cheffonier, sets of mahogany and painted chairs, capital swing glasses, wainscot and painted chests of drawers, dressing tables, wash stands, night conveniences, excellent wainscot wardrobe, sets of moreen window curtains, dinner and tea services, china and glass, sets of ivory-hafted knives and forks, mahogany dinner tray and stand, large dresser and pewter case, quantity of kitchen requisites, and other effects; which will appear in catalogues, to be had of the Auctioneers three days preceding the sale.

The Auctioneers beg to call the attention of the Public to the above sale, the Furniture, &c. having been purchased new within the last two years. Sale to commence precisely at Ten o'clock. *Stamford,* Jan. 14, 1846.

26. Adv. for furniture sale, *Mercury* 16 January 1846

largest bedroom, faced onto Scotgate. Both of these bedrooms had wooden shutters and black cast-iron fireplaces, most of which exist in the terrace today, albeit some have been painted in a different colour.   Finally, there was a small, single bedroom

27. Bedroom fireplace

with a window overlooking Scotgate, but without a fireplace. The bedrooms would have been more sparsely furnished than the living area below. The cupboards and wardrobes were more likely to have been made from wainscot, a variety of oak, which was less expensive than mahogany. The floors might be covered with reversible Brussels flat-weave rugs, or left bare, and the walls would be less adorned than in the living rooms below. The beds were the most important items on this floor, and the sale in 1846 indicates a four-poster in the main bedroom, a half-tester in the rear bedroom, and a French bed (equivalent to one and a half single beds) that would have fitted into the smallest bedroom.

Some servants, if lucky, may not have had to sleep in the kitchen, especially in the two houses with additional bedrooms on the second floor, or in the houses where there were few occupants. An example might have been Jane Burrows, one of the first servants to live in the newly built terrace. She was much older, and therefore more experienced, than a child maid-of-all-works, and as she lived alone with her spinster mistress, in no. 5, Jane may have been able to use a bedroom on the upper floor.

Externally, at the front, the terrace presents a uniform structure, and each house would have had cast-iron railings and gates set between the stone gate-piers. The buildings were constructed with small, coursed rubble, dressed with ashlared stone, the roofs are tiled with Welsh slate, and there are wide overhanging eaves, supported by wooden brackets and containing a lead-lined gutter. The entrance to each house is up a few external stone steps, and through a six-panelled door set in an arched, stone surround with a semi-circular fanlight above.

28. Eaves

Whilst there is uniformity in the internal layout of the houses, each rear garden is different in size and shape, be-cause the building plot was set within a triangle of land, and the gardens get progressively smaller as one moves from nos. 1 to 10. In addition, there are a couple of specific anoma-lies. The first is that the garden of no. 10 exits to the lane between the terrace and the spinney, whilst the rest exit to Rock Road. The second anomaly relates to the gardens of nos. 6 and 7, which were slightly restricted due to the steps leading down to the underground water pump. Previous structures on the Rock Terrace site were built on a quarry floor at the same level as Scotgate, and there was no access to the rear, which towered almost twenty feet above ground level. In order to provide rear access to the higher lane (now Rock Road) Newcomb built up the rear gardens at a gradient, which would have covered the precious pump. The solution was to build an underground, vaulted, brick room underneath the garden. This was rediscovered around 1970 when the council opened it up to investigate a blocked drain, then sadly filled it in and sealed it.

The unknown of 1842 is the exact location of the privy. It was obviously outside, but its initial location, or the type of privy, cannot be proven. It may have been an earth or ash latrine, where after each visit a layer of ash or earth covered the excrement, and which, when nearly full, was dug out and taken away by the night-soil men. Alternatively, the pail system may have been used, where large pails were placed under the privy seat, and again carried away by the night-soil men, but more regularly. One possible clue is in the coal room, the design of which cannot be explained. As shown in the floor plan, the room is L-shaped as one corner is missing. When excavated by some of the more recent occupants, to create extra space, possibly for a shower unit, it was discovered that this area was in fact a void.

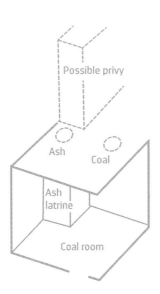

29. Possible privy and ash latrine pre-1864

It is possible that this was initially the site of an ash latrine. The closet seat could have been above or beside the pit, with a cover, through which to empty the daily ash, adjacent to the cover of the coal chute. This privy situation probably changed in 1864, when identical rear extensions were built to all houses. Again, there is no firm evidence to date these extensions, other than the fact that some 1865 advertisements for leases to nos. 9 and 10 stated that they had four bedrooms, whereas a year earlier only three were mentioned. The, roughly, seven-by eight-foot extensions were built over the basement coal room footprint, but also covered the void, and provided the ground and first floors with an additional room.

After the extension was built the occupants could pass through the original rear door into a room with a built-in store cupboard immediately to the left. This flowed to a new rear door to the garden, and immediately to the left was an outdoor brick-built privy, which by then was more than likely using the pail system and the night-soil service, which the local council continued to provide for many more years.

Above the ground floor extension was the new fourth bedroom, which was entered by a new narrow door that had been knocked through the original rear wall at the top of the staircase. The construction of the extension was different to the main house, which had very thick external walls, keeping it warmer in winter and cooler in summer. Instead, it was made of single brick to one side and the rear, and coursed rubble to the other side. Either immediately, or at a later date, the brick walls were rendered, again to all of the houses in the terrace, with the coursed rubble wall remaining exposed. Internally, the walls were battened, onto which was hung hessian, which was then papered. This rudimentary lining meant that this bedroom, without a fireplace, would have been particularly cold.

30. First floor extension door

The next change came around 1910, when all of the households, except one, no longer had live-in servants. Main sewage drains were finally added to the whole of the terrace and, for the first time, foul water from the scullery and sewage from the outside privy could be flushed away from the house. The drain started at no. 10, then ran down to no. 1, underground into the yard between nos. 30 and 31 Scotgate, and then left into Scotgate, where it joined the town's deep drain in the centre of the road. Once main drainage was operational, the extended first-floor rooms were gradually converted into bathrooms, but some not until as late as the end of the 1960s.

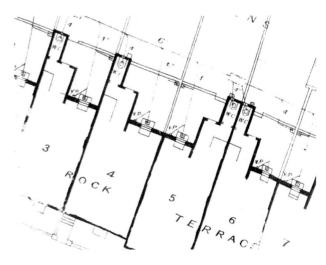

31. Section of drainage plan c.1910

When the terrace was sold en bloc in 1919, these rooms were described as box rooms, although prior to that these so-called fourth bedrooms may have been used as a servant's or companion's room. In the same sale particulars, it was noted that nos. 2, 5, 6, 9 and 10 had already converted these box rooms into bathrooms. The drainage plans of 1910 show internal doors to the outside WC, but it is possible that these were not converted from external to internal doors until after 1919, when the Potter family owned the terrace. It is rumoured that the builder R Ireson carried out this work.

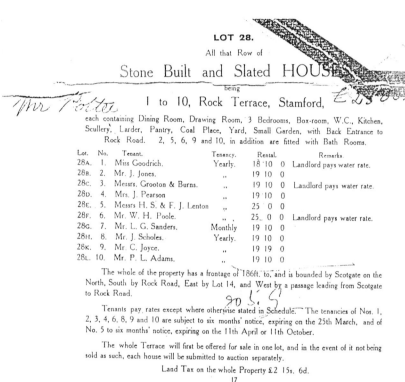

LOT 28.

All that Row of

Stone Built and Slated HOUSES

being

1 to 10, Rock Terrace, Stamford,

each containing Dining Room, Drawing Room, 3 Bedrooms, Box-room, W.C., Kitchen, Scullery, Larder, Pantry, Coal Place, Yard, Small Garden, with Back Entrance to Rock Road. 2, 5, 6, 9 and 10, in addition are fitted with Bath Rooms.

Lot.	No.	Tenant.	Tenancy.	Rental.	Remarks.
28A.	1.	Miss Goodrich.	Yearly.	18 10 0	Landlord pays water rate.
28B.	2.	Mr. J. Jones.	,,	19 10 0	
28C.	3.	Messrs. Grooton & Burns.	,,	19 10 0	Landlord pays water rate.
28D.	4.	Mrs. J. Pearson	,,	19 10 0	
28E.	5.	Messrs H. S. & F. J. Lenton	,,	25 0 0	
28F.	6.	Mr. W. H. Poole.	,,	25 0 0	Landlord pays water rate.
28G.	7.	Mr. L. G. Sanders.	Monthly	19 10 0	
28H.	8.	Mr. J. Scholes.	Yearly.	19 10 0	
28K.	9.	Mr. C. Joyce.	,,	19 19 0	
28L.	10.	Mr. P. L. Adams.	,,	19 10 0	

The whole of the property has a frontage of 186ft. to, and is bounded by Scotgate on the North, South by Rock Road, East by Lot 14, and West by a passage leading from Scotgate to Rock Road.

Tenants pay rates except where otherwise stated in Schedule. The tenancies of Nos. 1, 2, 3, 4, 6, 8, 9 and 10 are subject to six months' notice, expiring on the 25th March, and of No. 5 to six months' notice, expiring on the 11th April or 11th October.

The whole Terrace will first be offered for sale in one lot, and in the event of it not being sold as such, each house will be submitted to auction separately.

Land Tax on the whole Property £2 15s. 6d.

17

32. Sale particulars for Rock Terrace, 1919

By and large, these terraced houses remain the same today. There are layout differences, but all are recognisable as being of the same basic internal design. However, after the freeholds became available, from 1946, the new owners were free to make their own modifications, and it is these more recent changes that set the houses apart. The biggest contemporary modifications are the additions of garden rooms to the rear (most houses), the removal of the dividing wall between the pantry and the scullery (probably every house), the removal of the load-bearing wall between the pantry and the kitchen (some houses), and the removal of the larder room (a few houses). Where garden rooms have been added most of the rear ground floor WCs have been removed. In their stead, new WCs have been incorporated into what was the basement coal room, and in a few cases, as already mentioned, the void area in the old coal room has been dug out to make additional space for some to add a shower.

During the first hundred years of the terrace, save for the rear extensions, there were no external structural changes. Internally, changes and modifications were also minimal, partly due to the houses being under the control of landlords, and partly due to the social changes of the tenants, expanded in the following chapters. Typically, these terraced houses, built for the gentry and middle class, gradually became working-class homes with higher occupancy levels. Even though the freeholds started to be sold in 1946, the last was not sold until 1969, and one that was sold in 1967 had been largely untouched by modernising changes since 1865: there was no upstairs bathroom, nor electricity.

In the last fifty years, following the final freehold sale, a certain amount of re-gentrification has taken place, and currently the houses sell for almost three times the average house price in the UK. When the terrace was sold, in its entirety, in 1919, it fetched £2,500, and today the valuation total would exceed £6.5 million, a compound growth rate of around 8%

33. Rock Terrace watercolour by Graham Wright

CHAPTER 4

Early Tenants (1842–1866)

At the time that Newcomb built Rock Terrace, Queen Victoria was only a few years into her long reign, Martin Barry's New Palace of Westminster had just been completed, and the first postage stamps had come into use. Stamford was still an important coaching stop on the Great North Road, and barges continued to navigate the evermore silted-up River Welland, albeit with difficulty. Within Stamford's town walls a few cobbled streets were dimly lit by gas lamps at night but, without the town, the thoroughfares remained unpaved. Water was available from various pumps and wells in the town, and cesspits, open sewers and night-soil collection handled, ineffectively, the human waste.

Against this backdrop Newcomb had created a row of houses just outside the walls of the densely populated town, with water supplied daily from the pump, situated between 6 and 7 Rock Terrace. The additional benefit of a small garden and a rear entrance may have seemed an attractive proposition, but, at an annual rent of around £25, he had to find his first tenants.

It was unlikely to have been an easy task, due to the building work that continued for another three years at the northern end of Scotgate. Newcomb's builder, Robert Woolston, needed to complete the work on the terrace whilst demolishing Rock Cottage, and beginning to build, in its place, Newcomb's new primary residence, Rock House. This was followed by the final Newcomb development between Rock Terrace and the Green Man Inn.

As the work continued and new tenants were sought, the Stamford Victorians continued to be entertained by their fairs and freak shows. From the Middle Ages, Stamford has held a mid-Lent fair, and in 1842 there was the added attraction of a visit from Wombwell's touring menagerie. However, that year, one local man paid the price for getting too close to one of Wombwell's tigers, which attached itself to the man's arm. It took four men, and the application of hot irons to the tiger's nose, before a release was effected. The man's arm was badly injured, and the resulting pandemonium caused a stampede away from the menagerie. The Wombwell menagerie, or its derivations, returned to Stamford many times and years later the grandson of Henry Hayes, who had lived on the Browne's Hospital land, would marry into the

Wombwell family, and move into Rock Terrace.

By the end of that year, only two of the terraced houses had been let: one to Henry Jackson, a wine and spirits agent, and another to John Barratt, a piano tuner, who was also an agent for Broadwood pianos and who provided singing lessons from his new home. It was not until 1847 that each of the ten houses had had at least one tenant, and not until 1849 that the whole terrace was let at the same time. Other early tenants were Charles Copping and his wife Lucy. They had married at Whaplode on 13 February 1843, and immediately moved into 7 Rock Terrace. Tragically, a year later to the day, Lucy died. Charles returned to Whaplode, remarried, and continued his life as a farmer.

When Ann Anderson, the widow of Rev. Edward Anderson, the rector of St Luke's, Hickling, Nottinghamshire, moved into no. 5 in 1844, she became the first of a long list of single women of independent means who would reside in the gracious, but manageable, houses. Others quickly followed: the Mrs Clapham, Coverley, Newton, Smith and Jackson, respectively the widows of a surgeon, farmer, schoolmaster, draper, and landowner. The latter, Mrs Ann Jackson (see profile 3), was only in the terrace for a couple of years before dying at no. 9 in 1849, but she had led an interesting life, way beyond her initial expectations.

PROFILE 3

From 'below stairs' to Lady of the Manor

Ann Jackson (née Smith)   9 Rock Terrace 1848–1849

Ann Smith was born in Great Casterton in 1777. Little is known about her early life, other than she did not marry, and that her brother Richard, a cottager, remained in Great Casterton. However, as an unmarried young lady of her background, she would probably have gone into service.

By 1816, at the age of 39, Ann was part of the household at Duddington Manor, the family seat of the Jackson family, who were granted arms in 1688. Hugh Jackson and his wife, Jane, were the current occupants of the manor house, built by Hugh's ancestor, Nicholas, in 1633. Later in 1816, Jane, who had borne Hugh ten children, passed away and Ann, who was probably her lady's maid, or the Duddington Manor housekeeper, featured prominently at her funeral. Ann rode to the church in the third coach, a porte-chaise, together with Elizabeth Jackson, a daughter. Being granted the honour of riding in a carriage with a family member signified the position she must have held within the household, and her closeness to the deceased.

Hugh Jackson had been a well-known and eminent attorney in Stamford, but was now retired and managing his estate in Duddington, and properties elsewhere. Three years after Jane's death, Hugh, aged seventy-four, married Ann Smith, forty-two. It is difficult to identify the true circumstances of this morganatic marriage. Was Ann previously Hugh's mistress, was it for companionship and support in the autumn of Hugh's life, or was it a surprise romance which followed the death of Jane?

They were married discreetly, under licence, far away in Great Yarmouth, Norfolk, on 2 September 1819. The family were aware, as a marriage settlement had been drawn up, providing Ann with an allowance of £100 per annum, and protecting the rights of Hugh's children to inherit the manor estate. Hugh and Ann lived together at Duddington Manor, and in London, with Ann managing the household. By 1828, Ann was receiving £4 per week for household expenses, and an additional personal allowance of £7 10s. each quarter. Hugh's 1828 diary shows his handwriting deteriorating during the year, and he died on 28 April 1829, at Duddington.

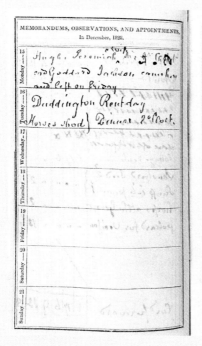

34. Hugh Jackson's diary, December 1828

In his will, he reaffirmed the marriage settlement, left Ann a legacy of £100, and provided her with the use of a cottage in Duddington, together with its garden, dovehouse and outbuildings, for the rest of her natural life, or whilst 'she shall think proper' to remain.

At Hugh's funeral, Ann travelled in the first coach with Hugh's son, Hugh Jackson of Wisbech, who was an executor of Hugh's will, which stipulated that the house, designated for Ann, be put into good repair. Whilst this was being carried out, Ann stayed with a friend in London, and it was there that she received some wine and £130 in bank notes (her legacy plus an extra gift from the executors) sent by Hugh from Wisbech. It is clear from her letter in response that she was very moved by 'the kind and generous attention' he had given her. In another sentence, suggesting that perhaps not all of the Jackson extended family had agreed with the marriage, she remarked 'I have allways felt since the death of your dear father that you was the only friend I had left'.

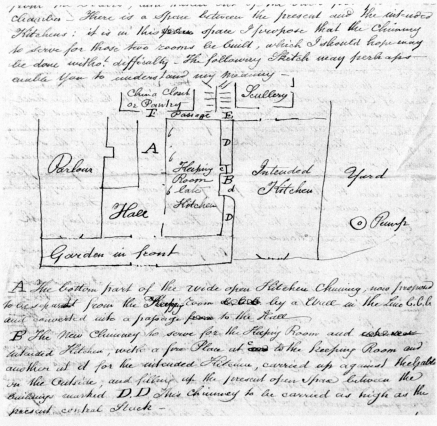

35. Instruction for the cottage renovation, Rev. J Jackson letter 1829

Ann subsequently moved to the house in Duddington, which had been renovated and extended on the advice of the Rev. Jeremiah Jackson, another of Hugh's sons. He had appointed Thomas White, a builder and architect with an office on Cowgate, Peterborough, to carry out the work. This involved moving a chimney from the centre of the house to the south gable end, and adding a single-storey kitchen to the side of the house. Until the middle of the twentieth century this delightful house was called 'The Cottage' but is now known as Braddan House, and the 1829 kitchen, which extends out to the pavement, remains clearly identifiable. Ann remained in Duddington until 1848, when she moved to 9 Rock Terrace where, in the following year, she died at the age of seventy-two.

36. Braddan House

Ann had moved from servant girl, to lady's maid or housekeeper, to wife of a gentleman, and in the process had accumulated enough wealth to warrant her own will. The Stamford solicitor who drew it up was Thomas Hippisley Jackson, one of her late husband's grandchildren, and in it, Ann was able to bequeath around £700 to a variety of Smith nieces and nephews.

In 1844, with Newcomb's Scotgate developments almost complete, the Stamford council resolved to place a street gas lamp outside of 3 Rock Terrace, occupied at that time by George Pearce, the organist at St Michael's church. Although the method of illumination has changed several times over the years, a street light has remained in the same spot ever since. Later that year there was great excitement in Stamford, when Queen Victoria and Prince Albert arrived en route to Burghley House where they were guests of the Marquess of Exeter. Crowds gathered in St Martin's to welcome the royal procession as it made its way from Duddington up to the lodge entrance of the house.

Widowers also found Rock Terrace a convenient and comfortable place to which to retire, with Robert Secker, gentleman, taking up residence at no. 2 in 1845, followed by John Roden in 1847. Roden was a retired draper and past mayor of Stamford, who together with his friend Richard Newcomb was, in 1826, made a JP for life. He died at his home in the terrace in 1849, aged sixty-six.

One Rock Terrace had remained unoccupied since its completion, and therefore, in 1845, was available for Richard Newcomb to house his new editor, John Paradise, who would become an important figure in Stamford, and for the *Mercury*. Paradise was the first of several *Mercury* employees who would reside in the terrace, or in other Newcomb-owned properties in the town. However, there is no evidence, as others have suggested, that any of the terrace houses, in particular the larger middle two properties, were reserved solely for *Mercury* staff (see Appendix 3). They may well have been given preference over other potential tenants, as having an employee as a tenant made good business sense, but given Newcomb's commercial nous it is unlikely they received a discount to the going rate. Certainly, in the 1900s, the Newcomb heirs were charging two *Mercury* employees exactly the same rent as other tenants in the terrace.

A year later, Paradise had to report on the outrage of Stamford inhabitants, as a result of the effluvium emanating from a new guano factory near the gas works. The factory was the latest project of Claudius Ludovicus Laségue, a native of Paris, who had arrived in Stamford via Lincoln in the late 1820s. Initially, he specialised in teaching French, but also gave lessons in Italian, dancing and fencing. In 1830, whilst living at 6 Rutland Terrace, he started selling a cure-all medicine called *Elixir Sans Pareil*. Apparently, this was made from a formula passed down from his grandfather, who had been a physician to Louis XVI of France. His advertisements often contained fulsome testimonials, and had the added benefit of stating that his remedy had been positively referenced in the *Lancet*.

After Newcomb had acquired the George and Angel from Browne's Hospital in 1843, Laségue became its landlord, running it together with his son, whilst continuing to give private language lessons and developing his guano project. Laségue became a partner with E Encontre, a Parisian chemist, who had filed, and obtained, a patent for making the fertiliser. Laségue had a free hand to develop the business, and arranged to have the night-soil scavengers of Stamford deliver the human faeces to his site near the gas works, where it would be mixed with a disinfectant and other materials, to reduce the odour and produce the fertiliser, called Perazote Guano. In September 1846, the stench was so bad that some tenants near the factory gave notice to quit, but at a subsequent meeting of the Stamford Improvement Commissioners, Laségue agreed to move the manure manufacturing further out of town, to Hudds Mill, and that settled the matter. The business continued until at least 1849, not least because it actually worked (the effluvium issue of 1846 was probably due to a manufacturing error), and was less than half the price of imported Peruvian Guano. However, Laségue never gave up his language lessons. He died at St Omer, in 1880.

The clergy, and family members of clergymen, were also well represented at the terrace during the early years. Mrs Ann Anderson, mentioned above; Miss Charlotte Twopenny (see profile 4), the daughter of the late Rev. Richard Twopenny of Little

Casterton; and the Rev. Ellis Bowden Were, the rector of St. Martin's, all moved in during 1844 and 1845. They were followed by the Rev. Edmund May, the newly appointed rector of St George's, and the Rev. James Edwin Tunmer, of the United Reformed Church in Star Lane, in 1848 and 1851.

PROFILE 4

A Vicar's Spinster Daughter

Charlotte Twopenny   No 6 Rock Terrace 1844–1848
                                  No 5 Rock Terrace 1849–1856

After the death of her father, the Rev. Richard Twopenny, in 1843, Charlotte, with an inherited annuity of £90, moved from the vicarage at Little Casterton to become the first tenant of 6 Rock Terrace. At a rent of at least £25 per annum, Charlotte probably had additional capital of her own in order to fund her new life in Stamford. In the preceding years she certainly had the ability to make donations, on her own account, to a number of causes. In 1835 Charlotte donated two guineas to help provide schools and chapels in the West Indies for 'emancipated negroes' following the Royal Assent of the Slavery Abolition Act the year before. The following year she subscribed £2 to the fund to rebuild St Michael's Church in Stamford and £1 to save the parish church of Friesthorpe.

Twenty years previously, her father had become embroiled in a spat with the local, and as yet unknown, poet John Clare. The Stamford bookseller Edward Drury had sent the Reverend some of Clare's poems for an opinion and the reply was that the poems 'possess no merit to be worthy of publishing'. Unwittingly Drury showed the Reverend's reply to Clare, who was hurt by the criticism and penned a witty riposte – a play on the surname Twopenny, ending 'And not care twopence about him'.

Charlotte's cousin, the lawyer and antiquarian, William Twopenny, was an avid artist of buildings of architectural interest. He did not live in Stamford, but during his visits he sketched some of the older buildings that no longer exist, and his son bequeathed many of his sketch books to the British Museum.

Charlotte either knew of, or became a friend of, her neighbour at no. 5, Ann Anderson. When Ann moved out of the terrace, at the end of 1848, Charlotte moved into her house, another of the larger properties in the middle of the terrace. She remained there until 1856, when, following the death of her sister-in-law, she moved to be with her brother in Dawlish. Jane Burrows (see profile 14, page 91), who was Charlotte's cook/housemaid also moved to Dawlish, returning to Stamford after Charlotte's death in 1878. Years later, some of Jane Burrows' nieces became tenants in Rock Terrace.

Stamford had been a stagecoach hub for many years, helped by its location on the Great North Road, and was an important stop for the twenty coaches north and twenty south each day on the London to York route. These coaches were a constant sight at Rock Terrace as they exited or entered the town, but this situation, and the associated economic benefits to Stamford, was not to last. The first nail in the coaching trade's coffin was the failure of Stamford to secure a position on the Great North railway line. This was followed, in 1847, with the opening of the Peterborough to Ely Railway which meant that it was possible to travel by train from Stamford to London, via Cambridge, and the loss of the coaching trade became terminal.

Newcomb had been an active member of the Stamford council and its committees for a number of years, and, in 1847, he became mayor of Stamford. It was a busy time for him. Besides the railway issues mentioned above, the old narrow bridge across the River Welland was demolished and the larger current bridge was built in its place. In July that year, Newcomb, as mayor, became the returning officer for the first general election in Stamford for fifteen years. Newcomb supported a Liberal candidate, John Rolt, who opposed the two Cecil family nominations, and who based his campaign around the uproar caused by the loss of the Great North line through Stamford. Newcomb did all he could to support Rolt, whose campaign headquarters was at Newcomb's Stamford Hotel. In addition, the Newcomb-owned Mason's Arms on Scotgate was renamed Rolt's Arms, and the local council provided Rolt with a lease for accommodation in Newcomb's Rock Terrace, probably no. 8. Rolt was unsuccessful in the election, but in later years became a Conservative MP, and went on to become attorney general in Lord Derby's government.

37. Rolts Arms, with the Clock House in the distance

Apart from the retirees and widows, younger active businessmen were also being attracted to the terrace, some as newly-weds and others as bachelors gaining residency prior to becoming married in the parish of All Saints'. One of these, Robert Michelson, had been working in the Uppingham office of the bankers Eaton, Cayley & Michelson, of which his father was a partner. In 1850, Robert (see profile 5) moved back to Stamford to join the head office of the bank, but also to marry. At the same time John Paradise, the *Mercury* editor, having outgrown 1 Rock Terrace, moved with his wife, eight children, and maid, to 24 St Mary's Street, another Newcomb property.

PROFILE 5

The Widower Banker

Robert Michelson   4 Rock Terrace 1850–1851

Whilst Robert was working at the Uppingham branch of Eaton, Cayley & Michelson, he met and courted Mary Keal, the daughter of a surgeon and devout Baptist from Oakham. They became engaged, and in 1850 Robert moved back to work in the Stamford office and live at no. 4, with his sister Jane Eliza. Although residing at the terrace for less than two years it was probably a time when he was at his happiest, contemplating a successful future life with his bride-to-be.

38. 2 St Mary's Place, from St Mary's churchyard

After their marriage in April 1851, the newly-weds set up home at 2 St Mary's Place, another of Richard Newcomb's properties and one of the most prestigious addresses in Stamford. Here, Mary apparently declared 'no more chapel for me' and, together with Robert, enjoyed a new carefree life, probably attending St Mary's Church, which their new home overlooked. Her disdain for chapel may have been influenced by the fact that her pastor in Oakham was the most well-known Strict Baptist, John Charles Philpott, whose sermons and writings are quoted to this day, especially in the USA.

In 1852, their first child, Mary Jane, was born, followed in 1853 by Charlotte Elizabeth and then in 1855 by Catherine Alexandra. Unfortunately, Catherine died within four months of her birth, beginning a turmoil in Robert's life which would persist.

In the autumn of 1856, Robert's wife, Mary, became ill with a slow, debilitating, pulmonary illness, which progressed until her death in August 1858. Following the death of their daughter Catherine, the Michelson's had found solace by returning to, and embracing, the Baptist faith, and began visiting the North Street Chapel in Stamford, where Philpott was also the alternating pastor. The renewal of their Baptist faith was a great comfort to them both during Mary's long decline and, in the end, it was Philpott who wrote a detailed obituary in the *Gospel Standard* describing her struggle.

39. North Street Chapel

As a Strict Baptist, Philpott did not pull any punches. He suggested that the death of the child and mother were God's will, following the relapse of Mary's faith. He wrote of the death of the child 'The Lord's gracious purposes, however, were ripening fast and the first intimation that he gave of his merciful intentions towards her was by removing her youngest child by death when about four months old, after a lingering illness'. And of Mary, he said 'but the Lord now began to lay his hand on her tabernacle and brought into her frame that disease which though at first scarcely perceptible, never released its hold, until after about two years languishing and suffering, it laid her body in the dust'.

After the death of his father in 1864, Robert was made a partner in the bank and moved to the bank's premises at 9 Broad Street. He became a local JP, never remarried, and in his retirement he lived initially at Bredcroft House, on Tinwell Road. Later, Robert moved into 1 Broad Street, a house vacated by his brother Henry, after his death in 1898. Robert remained in this house, until his death in 1902.

Until about 1849, Richard Newcomb and his staff at the *Mercury* managed the recruitment of tenants for the terrace, but thereafter Newcomb's solicitor took over.

However, this changed again following Newcomb's death in 1851. Richard's nephew, Robert Newcomb, inherited the estate and the management of the *Mercury*, which in turn led to the appointment of James Richardson, a local builder and auctioneer, to manage the properties and recruit new tenants.

In 1851, a thirty-year-old Samuel Weddell moved into 6 Rock Terrace. He had arrived in Stamford six years earlier, set up the Broad Street Academy, and by 1850 was employing none other than Monsieur C L Laségue to teach French. In December 1850 he sold the academy to Mr Thacker, which precipitated the move to Rock Terrace. For a couple of years he survived by giving art lessons at the house, then, in 1853, he set off for Australia with a cargo of goods, which he hoped would turn a good profit. Samuel's wife and children remained at no. 6 until he returned. By the end of 1854 Samuel had opened a new school at 51 High Street, another of the Newcomb properties. This house had reputedly been owned by Octavius Gilchrist, the editor of a rival newspaper, with whom Newcomb had fought a duel in 1812. It would seem that Newcomb may have obtained a certain amount of pleasure in buying up this property, as well as Rock Cottage, both homes of previous adversaries. Unfortunately, this historic building, originating from the Middle Ages and trading as the Windmill Inn in the eighteenth century, was demolished in 1966, a year before Stamford became a conservation town. In its place, adjacent to what was the National Westminster Bank, stands a contender for the most uninspiring building on the High Street.

40. 51 High Street

Another widow, Mary Knight, moved into the terrace in 1851: the mother of Richard Knight, a prominent businessman, and one of Stamford's Improvement Commissioners. Mary Knight's husband had sold his business in Osgodby in 1817 to lead a life of semi-retirement, and in 1820 probably financed his twenty-one-year-old son to become a partner with Mr Beasley, who ran a linen and drapery business. The business became known as Beasley & Knight, and traded from large premises on the corner of the High Street and Ironmonger Street (now Café Black).

In 1823, Richard bought out Beasley, who in turn bought out Alderman Edward Butt, another draper on the High Street, and the two became competitors.

Butt died in 1834, and his son Francis was the mayor who died in the hunting accident in 1839, leading to Newcomb obtaining the Scotgate land. When Richard Knight's father died, also in 1839, he was buried at his birthplace of Lenton, and Mary continued to live on Broad Street and work with her son as a draper until she retired. Mary lived at 3 Rock Terrace until her death in 1863.

41. Site of Knight's drapery shop

During the 1850s there were signs that tenancies in the terrace were becoming more settled, and lasting much longer. This may or may not be due to the property management changes, but those moving into the terrace during this time, and staying for more than five years, included Joseph Wilson, silversmith; Mrs Mary Knight, the widow mentioned above; Mrs Elizabeth Priestley, widow; William Knight, coal waggoner; John Charles Ridgway, music teacher; George Baker, retired chemist; and Mrs Lucy Pepper, widow.

Joseph Thomas Wilson was the son of a master silversmith, and was himself a silversmith and jeweller. In 1850, he married Fanny Webster, the daughter of a wealthy landowner, and made 2 Rock Terrace his first marital home. Their first child was born at the house in 1851, and also residing with the family at that time were Joseph's widowed mother-in-law, a nurse, and a servant girl.

Joseph's father, Joseph Snr, ran a very successful jewellery and watchmaking business in All Saints' Place, which he started in 1818. Joseph was born in 1823, but his mother died in 1836, and his father was remarried in 1839 to Mary Ann Holmes, a widow. In 1840, Joseph Snr bought the freehold of his shop, workshop and living accommodation at 9 All Saints' Place. He also acquired 10 All Saints' Place, which together with no. 9 became the site for the Stamford Post Office, and a house on Horse Shoe Lane, currently the site occupied by the Cosy Club café.

When Joseph Snr died in 1855 he left a detailed will, which granted Mary Ann a life interest in his properties that would pass to Joseph on her death. Joseph, who had been working with his father, became the proprietor of the family business and, together with Fanny and his three children, moved into the spacious accommodation above the shop, together with his stepmother, mother-in-law, and various servants and shop staff. On 18 September 1855, much of Joseph and Fanny's furniture was sold in an auction at 2 Rock Terrace: rosewood and mahogany pieces, including a crimson-covered sofa, similar to items sold from no. 8 in 1846. Fanny was now the business owner's wife and may have wanted to take the opportunity of buying some of the latest and more fashionable furniture. As a Victorian wife, she would have wanted to provide her husband with a more modern household, where, by 1861, she had dutifully borne him another four children.

In March 1854, Britain and France declared war on Russia, and the Crimean War began. By then Henry Hayes, the wheelwright who had occupied part of the land on which Rock Terrace was built, had developed a thriving cart and carriage-making business with his son, John, and they became the first such company to be awarded a government contract to supply wagons to support the war effort. Later that year James Brudenell, 7th Earl of Cardigan, whose family seat, Deene Park, is situated close to Stamford, led the Charge of the Light Brigade at the Battle of Balaclava.

Also in 1854, John Ridgway moved into 9 Rock Terrace, where his third child, who unfortunately only survived a few months, was born. He had been a Professor of Music in London and, in 1851, moved north to marry Eliza Nelsey and live in Spalding, where their first two children were born. They left Stamford and settled in Peterborough where, in 1859, they had their fourth child, but later that year John drowned whilst swimming with a friend in a nearby river. He had been under his doctor's care, due to a weak heart, and had been cautioned not to exert himself. The inquest jury decided, 'That deceased had been bathing in the Nene, and being in a weak state of health fell into the river and died by suffocation from water'. He was only thirty and left a widow and three young children. Eliza was relatively lucky, as to be widowed so young, without capital, and without another male to take care of her and her children, she may have become destitute very quickly. However, she moved to Great Yarmouth and took in lodgers, then later moved to Southampton where she ran a boarding house, and during this time was able to successfully bring up and educate her children. She died in Southampton at the age of fifty-nine.

In 1859, the new Corn Exchange was opened on Broad Street and two early performances, confirming the Victorians continued interest in the extraordinary, were given by Tom Thumb, the American dwarf, and Picco, the blind Sardinian minstrel. Later that year, and even more extraordinary in post-Industrial-Revolution England, was the sighting, from Stamford's higher ground, of the aurora borealis.

In the same year, Charles Darwin published his long-awaited *Origin of the Species*. It had a long gestation as Darwin's voyage on HMS *Beagle*, as far as Tierra del Fuego took place between 1831 and 1836 – before Rock Terrace was ever contemplated. Back in 1825, Darwin had corresponded with the Rev. Lansdown Guilding, who lived on the island of St Vincent and as a botanist was able to provide Darwin with notes on Caribbean species. Guilding was married to Mary Hunt, the daughter of Rev. Samuel Hunt of St George's Church in Stamford, and their daughter Sarah would later move to England, and eventually live at Rock Terrace (see profile 7).

Twenty years after Newcomb had developed the upper end of Scotgate little in Stamford had changed. It remained overcrowded and unsanitary, and although by 1839 more than four thousand enclosure acts had been passed in the UK, Stamford's Enclosure Act, which would enable housing development on the fields north of the town wall, would not become effective until 1875.

As was becoming evident in the 1850s, the terrace was filling with tenants who would remain for many years. One of these, Mrs Eliza Syson, moved into no. 1 in 1863, and remained there until her death in 1889 at the age of eighty-one. Eliza had previous experience of living at Rock Terrace as, in 1851/52, she rented no. 9, when her two boys started at Stamford School. In 1848, her husband William Baines Syson, a gentleman farmer, was killed in a shooting accident at Burley-on-the-Hill and, although she kept their farm near Oakham, Eliza decided to be closer to her children during their formative years. Alfred, the eldest boy, was admitted to Christ College, Cambridge in 1860, but in March 1861 he died of typhus, a flea borne infection, whilst at the university. Prince Albert died of the similarly named typhoid fever, a food borne infection, later that year. Alfred's brother, Andrew, was admitted to Clare College, Cambridge in 1864 and went on to become a priest. Within two years of the death of Alfred, Eliza moved out of the farm and settled permanently in Stamford.

Another who moved into the terrace, at the same time as Eliza, was George Dewse. When Robert Nicholas Newcomb died in 1863, and the proprietorship of the *Mercury* passed to his mother, Sarah, she appointed George as head clerk to manage the paper, whilst John Paradise continued admirably as its editor. Initially, George took up residence at no. 10, a property that seemed in the future to be reserved for shorter tenancies. However, in 1865, when it became vacant, he moved to no. 5, one of the larger middle properties with six bedrooms.

John Paradise, whilst editor of the *Mercury*, was elected mayor of Stamford in 1864, and was still living at 24 St Mary's Street, the Newcomb owned house which was more suited for his large family, and with the added advantage of being around the corner from the *Mercury* office.

42. 24 St Mary's Street

Across town, on Broad Street, the Dolphin Inn had been demolished, and the new Roman Catholic Church of St Augustine built in its stead. It was opened in June 1865, with the celebration of a full pontifical Mass, the first to be performed in Stamford since the reformation. A year later, catering to the public in a less serious way, saw the return of Tom Thumb, now married, who during his visit was invited, with his wife, to Burghley House as guests of the Marquess. A month later, Chang, the 7 ft 10 in. Chinese giant, together with his entourage, also travelled to Stamford to entertain the locals.

In November 1866, Sarah Newcomb died at Stibbington House, and the contents of her will was met with surprise and dismay by the Newcomb family and the wider public in Stamford. The custodianship of the *Mercury*, and all of the property assets of the Newcomb estate, were bequeathed to her nephew, John Todd, a Cumbrian farmer. The fact that the prior will of her son, Robert, had stipulated that any future heirs could only inherit if they changed their name to Newcomb, did not assuage the Newcomb family members, who had been ignored, but it did provide an additional legacy of the Newcomb name. John dutifully obliged by changing his name to John Todd-Newcomb, and the formal announcement appeared in the *London Gazette* on 1 February 1867 and the *Edinburgh Gazette* a few days later, which also seemed to confirm Richard Newcomb's right to bear arms.

> **WHITEHALL, January 24, 1867.**
>
> The Queen has been pleased to give and grant unto John Todd, of Guards, in the parish of Kirby Irleth, in the county of Lancaster, Esquire, Her royal licence and authority that he may, in compliance with a clause contained in the last will and testament of Robert Nicholas Newcomb, of Stamford, in the county of Lincoln, Esquire, deceased, take and henceforth use the surname of Newcomb, in addition to and after that of Todd, and bear the arms of Newcomb quarterly with those of Todd, and that the said surname and arms may be so taken and borne by his issue; such arms being first duly exemplified according to the laws of arms and recorded in the College of Arms, otherwise the said royal licence and permission to be void and of none effect;
>
> And also to command that the said Royal concession and declaration be recorded in Her Majesty's College of Arms.

43. Name change, Edinburgh Gazette 5 February 1867

CHAPTER 5

Longevity Tenants (1867–1887)

The loss of the stage coaching business, as a result of the introduction of the rail-way, continued its devastating impact on the town as outward migration of its inhabitants, looking for employment, had reduced the population of Stamford. The employment situation had been exacerbated by the Cecil family – Luddites who had refused to allow the railway from London to pass through Stamford, and who controlled the majority of land outside of the town walls, which could have been used for housing and industrial development. But a series of events which started with the death of Brownlow Cecil, the 2nd Marquess of Exeter, in 1867 and ended with Stamford's 1871 Enclosure Act, eventually reversed the town's decline. Brownlow Cecil had died on the eve of the assent of the 1867 Reform Act, which reduced Stamford's parliamentary seats to one, and Stamford's time as a pocket borough, whose inhabitants had been controlled by the Cecil family for so long, came to an end.

John Todd-Newcomb, who had changed his name only a couple of years before, died suddenly in 1868, and as his son and heir, Robert Nicholas Todd-Newcomb, was only two years old, the estate was managed by trustees for the next twenty years. Under trustee management, John Paradise remained as editor of the *Mercury*, and John Foster Overbury was appointed sub-editor. Initially, Overbury lived at 10 Rock Terrace, but, when it became vacant, he moved with his family into the larger no. 5. At the same time, Paradise's son, John Worsley Paradise, was living at 9 Rock Terrace and working as a newspaper reporter. However, by 1871 John Worsley had forsaken journalism to become a coal merchant and was living at 2 St Mary's Place.

The 1860s saw innovation and change in the capital: the first flushing toilet, the first tram, and the first underground train. However, little modernisation had reached Stamford where the roads needed daily watering to reduce the dust, and where the council were years away from considering mains drainage and the supply of piped water.

In 1869, the mayoralty of Stamford was taken by Garmston Chapman, who was living at 2 Rock Terrace. Garmston had, in 1824, bought a draper's shop, together with a counting house and warehouse, at 3 High Street (now the site of the clothing shop Crew). He lived there with his family and staff until he retired in 1855 and moved to the terrace.

In 1859, one of the grandest banquets seen in Stamford for many years was hosted by the new mayor, Octavius Simpson, for 250 guests. Garmston had been invited to respond to the toast proposed by Lord Robert Cecil for 'The Town and Trade of Stamford'. After praising the tradespeople of Stamford, Garmston commented that those present had 'witnessed as fine a specimen of old English hospitality as ever could be wished for'.

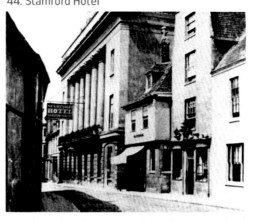
44. Stamford Hotel

The extensive menu, which was prepared at the Stamford Hotel and walked across the road to the town hall contained:

Soup, Fish etc.	12 Tureens of soup;	turtle, oxtail, julienne, vermicelli
	12 Side dishes of fish;	codfish, turbot, soles, fried eels, stewed eels
	Sauces;	shrimp, lobster, oyster
	Potatoes	
Removes	3 haunches of venison, 3 saddles of mutton, 3 joints of roast beef, 3 quarters of lamb, 6 dishes of geese, 6 dishes of ducks, 6 dishes of roast fowl, 6 dishes of boiled fowl, 3 galantines, 3 dishes of spiced beef, 3 hams, 6 tongues, 6 pigeon pies and 6 lobster salads.	
Second Service	6 dishes of grouse, 12 dishes of partridge, 6 dishes of roast hare, 6 dishes of gateaux napolitain, 6 dishes of gateaux savoie, 5 dishes of gateaux faurré, 12 dishes of jellies, 12 dishes of blanc manges and creams, 6 dishes of tartelettes of jam, 12 dishes of pastry.	
Dessert	Pines, grapes, melons, filberts, peaches, apricots, nectarines, walnuts, plums, apples, pears, crystallised fruit, preserved fruit, ratafias, rout cakes, and savoys.	
Wines	Sherry, hock, moselle, sauternes, madeira, champagne, port, claret etc.	

During his life Chapman had also been a councillor, an alderman and a JP. He died at the house on 18 June 1872. Ten days earlier Garmston had been sitting as a JP at the Stamford petty sessions, and seven days after his death Stamford Town Council held a special meeting to fill the aldermanic vacancy. At the meeting it fell to Alderman John Paradise, a previous Rock Terrace resident, to propose a vote of condolence to Garmston's widow. In doing so, Paradise included a most eloquent tribute to his former colleague and friend which was reported in the *Mercury* of 27 June 1872:

> … He did not think there was a person in that hall who had been personally antagonistic to the late Alderman, and he knew there were many who respected him as much as he did – as a man of conciliatory disposition, conscientious in his actions; ready to do anyone a kindness to the utmost extent of his power, and diligent in the discharge of his public duties. He found from a memorandum kindly noted by the Town Clerk that for more than a quarter of a century, off and on, he had been connected with the Corporation; and during the whole of the time, it might be said, scarcely an angry word had passed his lips in that hall; or if he had even been mixed up with the broils which sometimes disturbed the equanimity of the Council, and which now and then crept into the best-regulated and most aristocratic assemblies, it had been in the greatest possible form and without a trace of bitter feeling behind. His Mayoralty, as most of them know, was a peaceful one from the commencement to its close. On the bench where he knew Mr Chapman more intimately, he was constant in his attention to magisterial business and as one of his colleagues he could say most sincerely that his constant aim was to do strict justice without fear, favour or prejudice …

45. St Augustine's belfry

The new Catholic church in Broad Street was not complete when it was consecrated in 1865, as it was without a belfry and external adornments. In 1871 this was rectified when Thomas Charity Halliday, builder, and William Hilliam, sculptor, were taken on to build a campanile, install a bell, and enhance the exterior with perforated stonework and sculpted cornices. Later, the sons of both Halliday and Hilliam would live in Rock Terrace; Samuel Fancourt Halliday (see profile 10, page 77) would live at no. 9 and become mayor, and John William Hilliam, a stonemason, would spend a couple of years at no. 10.

Whilst William Hilliam was working on the church his father, John, a jour-
neyman mason, had returned to Stamford and was living at the Glaziers' Arms on
Scotgate with his second wife, Ann. John and Ann had a volatile, alcohol-fuelled relationship, and Ann in particular had been, and continued to be, an embarrassment
to her stepson. In 1859, the year of her marriage to John, Ann had been brought
before Stamford petty sessions for being drunk on no less than six occasions. Between 1860 and 1869, John and Ann were living in Melton Mowbray and Leicester,
but were again regulars in court: Ann was gaoled nine times, and John once. In the
worst case, which had to be escalated to Leicester assizes, Ann was found guilty of
housebreaking and larceny, and sentenced to two months hard labour. Drink caused
Ann to become violent and use foul language, and John became estranged from her
on several occasions, but in 1871 they were back together and living in Stamford.

However, in 1874, Ann was again before the local petty sessions for drunkenness
and using disgusting language, and twice sentenced to twenty-one days, the latter
with hard labour. Immediately on her return from gaol she was found drunk yet
again, and this time had to find two sureties of £5, and was bound over not to repeat.
But, repeat she did: the third parties lost their sureties, and it seems that Ann fled the
town. John's son and grandson, reputable masons in Stamford, probably distanced
themselves from the troublesome couple, and in 1875 John died alone in the Stamford Union workhouse.

In 1873, Mrs Elizabeth Kenrick (see profile 6) moved into 2 Rock Terrace, after
living for a while with her son at Great Casterton and, at the same time, spinster Sarah Jane Guilding (see profile 7) followed commercial traveller Henry Peake into no.
3. That year, Horace Wright, a baker, whose shop and accommodation was at 8 All
Saints' Place, next to Joseph Wilson's jewellery business, became mayor, and many
years later Horace's widow, Minnie, would move into 2 Rock Terrace.

Although the Stamford Enclosure Act had been passed by Parliament in 1871, it
did not take effect until 1875, when one of the largest parcels of land, fields to the
north of the town, was granted to the churchwarden of St George's. It was quickly
bought by the Stamford Freehold Land Society, whose trustees included John Paradise, the *Mercury* editor, and Edward Browning, a renowned local architect, who had
been mayor in 1863. The Rev. Henry Bayley Browning, the brother of Edward, was
the incumbent of St George's at the time, and later became Confrater of Browne's
Hospital. The land was divided up and plots sold off individually, creating what is
now the Northfields area of Stamford, bordered by New Cross, Kings and Alexandra
Roads, and Emlyn's Street.

46. Sale of plots at Northfields
29 November 1875 and signature
of John Paradise

PROFILE 6

Widowed by Suicide

Elizabeth Kenrick   2 Rock Terrace 1873–1889

Elizabeth Kenrick arrived at Rock Terrace in 1873 where she would remain, together with her faithful servant and companion, Rebecca Veal, for the rest of her life.

Twenty years previously Elizabeth had been living a very comfortable life at Frampton Villa, in Lincolnshire, with her husband Buxton Kenrick and their four children. Buxton was a solicitor, had previously been the town clerk of Boston, and was involved in a number of businesses including ship-owning. However, the big house with five servants, a coachman and a footman, were to become the casualty of Buxton's misfortune. He had overstretched himself and, heading for bankruptcy, Buxton absconded to Europe. This was most likely with the full knowledge of his family as, during the bankruptcy meetings which followed, it became evident that some of Buxton's assets had disappeared. So unreliable was the testimony of Rebecca Veal regarding some plate which had disappeared from the house that it was thought that she might be prosecuted for perjury.

Buxton never appeared at any of the hearings and an order was made for his arrest. He had accumulated debts in excess of £3,000, and his creditors never received dividends of more than a quarter of that sum.

The family were aware of Buxton's location in Europe and provided him with financial support as he built a new business in Lyon. After six years in France, his new enterprise was declared insolvent and the article below from the *Mercury*, taken from a report by the Naples correspondent of the *Morning Post*, takes up his story.

> … [Buxton] left France to join Garibaldi's legion, which was then besieging Capua. It appears that Mr. Kenrick on this occasion fell in with Miss Gray, a misguided young lady, although belonging to a respectable family, with whom he had previously been intimate in England. How or why she was in Naples is not clearly specified, but she immediately joined Mr. Kenrick there, and came on with him to Rome; but on account of this liaison, Mr. Kenrick's usual remittances from his wife's relations were suspended. Their circumstances, therefore, became more and more embarrassed, until they resorted to the last desperate expedient of suicide. They must have gone to the public garden of the Villa Beale, at Naples. There, the café being still open, they took a glass of rum or rosolio [a rose petal liqueur]. They then climbed over the low wall of the villa, where a semi-circular space over-looking the sea is furnished with stone steps and descended on the beach, where Miss Gray tied her dress round her ankles, and filled it with sand. Mr Kenrick effecting the same purpose by filling the bosom of his shirt, his waistcoat, and coat sleeves with sand and stones, Miss Gray supplying the necessary strings and tapes from her own dress. They then tied themselves together round the waist with their pocket-handkerchiefs, and deliberately lay down to die in the sea, which at that point is not more than two or three feet deep...

Following Buxton's disappearance, Elizabeth had moved to a more moderate house on Spilsby Road, Boston, and then to her son John's farmhouse in Great Casterton where Rebecca Veal, who had remained with the family for over thirty years, was also the housekeeper.

When her son John married at the end of 1871, Elizabeth and Rebecca took up residence at Rock Terrace, where they lived together until Rebecca died in 1887, aged eighty-seven, and Elizabeth a year later, aged eighty-one. Following Elizabeth's death another son, Buxton Martin Kenrick, a retired army captain, moved into the house, but his stay was short-lived, as he died on 25 January 1889.

George Baker was one of the longest continuous tenants, residing at 7 Rock Terrace for twenty-six years. He had been a well-known chemist in St Mary's Street, until he retired in 1853 and moved to the terrace. His first wife, Rebecca, had died five years earlier so he took up residence as a widower. In 1863, he married a widow, Margaret Reid Lunn, seventeen years his junior, and six years later was appointed a JP, under the mayoralty of his neighbour Garmston Chapman. Despite the age difference, George's second wife pre-deceased him in 1876, and George followed in 1879.

Tenants were not only remaining longer in the terrace, but also living longer. George Baker was eighty-three when he died, and was one of a number of tenants with extreme longevity for the time. In the 1870s, life expectancy at birth was around forty-one, but the low number was skewed by the high rate of infant mortality. If a person reached adulthood, his or her life expectancy would be closer to sixty. Even with this adjustment some tenants, including George, born much earlier between 1776 and 1806, reached venerable ages. The others were Eliza Syson who lived until she was eighty-one; Elizabeth Kenrick, eighty-three; Mary Knight, eighty-five; and Lucy Pepper, eighty-seven.

PROFILE 7

The Socialite Spinster

Sarah Jane Guilding   3 Rock Terrace 1873–1878

Sarah was born in 1821 on the island of St. Vincent. Her father was the Rev. Lansdown Guilding and her mother, Mary Hunt, was the daughter of the Rev. Samuel Hunt of St George's, Stamford.

47. St Vincent Botanic Garden, example of Guilding's artistry

Although born in St Vincent, her father had been sent to England as a five-year-old to be educated, and returned fifteen years later with a degree from Oxford. He immediately began collecting botanical specimens and a year later, in 1818, was accepted as a Fellow of the Linnean Society of London, the world's oldest surviving natural history society.

Lansdown developed his skills as an artist and lithographer enabling him to catalogue plants and insects in detail, and in rich colour.

In 1827, Sarah's mother died during the birth of her brother Edward. Her father remarried at the end of 1828, but three years later he died unexpectedly at the age of thirty-three. His botanical interests had taken precedence over the provision for his wife and six children, and his brother John and second wife Charlotte had to make attempts to sell Lansdown's books, manuscripts, paintings and lithographs in London. Sarah was brought up in St. Vincent, together with her full and half-siblings, other than Edward who was sent back to school in London. Eventually, the children migrated back to the UK and, as a young lady, Sarah moved permanently to Stamford, initially living with her uncle Edward Lindsell, and later as a companion to her aunt, Jane Hunt, at 39 High Street, St Martin's.

Sarah became part of Stamford society, attending the annual Dorcas Ball at the Assembly Rooms and eventually taking an active part in the fundraising for the Dorcas charity, set up in 1816 to provide clothing for the poor. The Assembly Rooms in Stamford were built in 1726 and today are the longest continually used set of rooms in England. In 1852, Sarah attended the ball hosted by the Marquess of Exeter, in the presence of the nobility and gentry of Stamford and beyond. Dancing commenced at nine-thirty and after six quadrilles, six waltzes, four polkas, two galops, one boulanger and one country dance the ball concluded at four-thirty the following morning. Also attending the ball was a neighbour at Rock Terrace – Miss Twopenny.

After her aunt died, Sarah moved to Rock Terrace. She knew the houses through her sister, Mary Anne, and late brother-in-law, Thomas Wingfield Hunt, who had briefly lived at no. 10 in 1867/1868. Thomas had been an assistant commissioner for the East India Company in Bengal, and in August 1868 Mary Anne left the terrace and travelled back to India with their children to be reunited with him. However, she was unaware that her husband had died suddenly in Akyab, Bengal on 7 August. After arriving to the devastating news, Mary Anne sorted out her husband's affairs, and by 1871 had returned with her children to England. A couple of years later she was living with her sister Sarah at 3 Rock Terrace.

Mary Anne died a few years later at the age of forty-nine, and when Sarah died in 1879, Mary Anne's children, Alice and George, who was a student for Holy Orders, moved into no. 8 where they remained until 1881.

About ten years into the trusteeship of the New-comb estate (the heir, Robert Todd-Newcomb, was still only twelve) the trustees decided to utilise the land previously designated by Richard Newcomb to build a new school. By 1879 two rows of ten terraced houses, facing each other, were built off St Leonard's Street and named Cornstall Buildings. Although widely reported in the past that these were built for *Mercury* employees, it seems that never more than five of the twenty houses, at any one time, were used for that purpose. Like Richard Newcomb before

48. Cornstall Buildings

them, the trustees saw a commercial opportunity, they took advantage of land they already owned, built twenty-much needed small houses in the centre of town, and probably promoted themselves as building houses for their employees.

After Sarah Guilding died in 1879, her place was taken by newly-weds Albert and Margaret Hayes (see profile 8). Ironically, almost forty years earlier, Albert's grandfather, Henry, had been moved from his dwelling and wheelwright's barn to

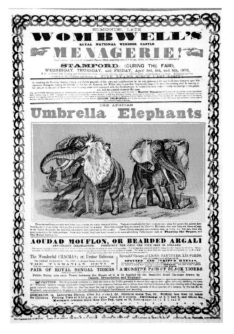

49. Adv. for Wombwell's Menag-erie, Stamford April 1878

make way for the building of the terrace. Henry Hayes had moved to Stamford in the late 1820s and besides plying his trade as a wheelwright was also, in 1831, the landlord of the Shepherd and Shepherdess public house on Castle Street. His time at the inn came to an end in 1838, when he was declared bankrupt, and he moved to Scotgate, where he had his workshop and lived in one of the tenements. Newcomb moved him out of that site and provided him with new premises across the road, alongside Britton's Court.

The relationship between Albert Hayes and Margaret Edmonds may have been kindled through a business relationship between Hayes & Son, coachbuilders, and Wombwell's second menagerie, which had been bequeathed to Margaret's mother. The Wombwell's menageries had used Hayes to build sturdy cages with which to transport their large, and often dangerous, wild animals from fair to fair. Wombwell's visited Stamford's mid-Lent fair in 1878, and Margaret, who assisted with the menagerie, was then twenty-seven. Albert and Margaret married the following year in London.

Stamford Coachbuilding Family

Albert Henry Hayes 3 Rock Terrace 1879–1885

Margaret Emma Hayes 10 Rock Terrace 1922–1924

By the time Albert was born in 1847, his father, John, had completed his wheelwright's apprenticeship and become a full partner with his father, trading as Hayes & Son. John became the dominant driver of the business, which became extremely successful over the next fifty years. The Hayes & Son success enabled John to send Albert to a boarding school in Northampton, under the tutelage of William Kingston, after which he joined the family business.

Early success was based on the provision of wagons and carts, and by the 1860s they had outgrown their worksite at the town end of Scotgate. In order to continue to expand, John acquired the carriage-making business of Abraham Allen in Peterborough, and whilst maintaining the knowledge-base of Allen, nineteen-year-old Albert moved to Peterborough to supervise. He lived there for over a decade, during which time he became the works manager, and joined St Peter's masonic lodge.

50. Margaret and Albert Hayes, c. 1900

As Hayes & Son moved into the more sophisticated carriage-building business, their wagons, not least for the wars in the 1870s, remained in demand. At the same time, through one of their more unusual clients, Albert met and married Margaret Edmonds. Margaret provided Albert with a large family of six boys, but after the third was born, 3 Rock Terrace was no longer big enough for them, and in 1886 the family moved to 10 St Peter's Hill, where they had their own carriage entrance.

Hayes & Son continued expand, and in 1878 John purchased the ironworks on Scotgate, and together with his land on West Street consolidated all of his Stamford manufacturing onto a single site, which is now a town car park. In 1884, John acquired a site in London and began manufacturing there to satisfy that large and lucrative market. During this time, John

Hayes was a continuous public servant, sitting on the Stamford council from 1876, and was twice elected mayor, as well as being a prominent Freemason of the Stamford lodge.

51. Adv. for Hayes & Sons carriages

When John retired in 1894, Albert took over the business and was joined by his brother, John Edey Hayes, who had been a banker. Albert was responsible for the Stamford and Peterborough works, whilst John looked after the London business. A spat between the brothers led to the end of their filial relationship, and some family members believe that it led to the death of John Edey, in 1904. A few years later Albert became ill, eventually dying in 1910. Both sons were outlived by their father, who died in 1916. In 1921, a fire ripped through the Scotgate works and even though the family built a new office block, and repaired the damage, the business ceased three years later.

Margaret, whom a family member believes was rudely described in Stamford as 'the largest woman with the smallest brain in town' was, in 1911, living at 13 Rutland Terrace with two of her adult boys. She was born in 1851, in a caravan at Midsomer Norton, Somerset, and spent years travelling with her parents' menagerie, which contained 'some of the most beautiful groups of trained lions, panthers, leopards and tigers'. Now she resided at this prestigious terrace which had a commanding view across the fields towards the Bottle Lodge entrance to Burghley House.

In 1922, Margaret moved back to Rock Terrace. It was a brief sojourn at no. 10, the house that seemed to be used for short-term tenants, as she lived at 3 Emlyn's Street from the end of 1924, until she died in 1930.

On 15 January 1881, the Prince and Princess of Wales were guests of the Marquess of Exeter at Burghley House. The previous day had been spent at Normanton and the royal party made their way to Burghley via Scotgate, which was decked out with bunting and flags. The *Mercury* reported 'in front of Mr Halliday's house in Rock Terrace [no. 9] were a couple of evergreen-clad poles, bearing the royal standard, and other effective decorative devices'.

Two months later Alexander II, Czar of Russia, who had been a guest of the young Queen Victoria in 1838, was assassinated in St Petersburg. The bullet-proof carriage, a gift from Napoleon III, was not a match for the bomb that was exploded near the Pevchensky Bridge, only a couple of miles from the home of Elizabeth Grotten, who within a few years would return to Stamford. The following year, in 1882, Queen Victoria suffered her eighth, and last, attempted assassination. After arriving at Windsor station, she was being transferred to Windsor Castle in her carriage when Roderick Maclean fired a pistol. He was quickly overcome by Eton schoolboys, who had gone to the station to greet the Queen, and later Maclean was judged to be mentally ill and sent to an asylum.

52. John Hayes, 1882

The annual Dorcas Ball, at the Assembly Rooms, was still able to attract a large gathering of England's nobility and gentry, under the patronage of the Marquess of Exeter. In 1882, leading politicians, including Lord Randolph Churchill, Sir Stafford Northcote and Lord Burghley, were amongst the 250 guests, which included, by dint of his position as mayor of Stamford, John Hayes, the wheelwright's son.

Later that year, Queen Victoria gave her assent to the Married Women's Property Act, 1882. This provided a major improvement in both the rights and status of women in England. Until this Act, which commenced on 1 January 1883, a woman, upon marriage, became a non-person, merely a chattel of her husband. It followed that because she was not a legal person she could not own property. From 1883, a married woman was able to keep inherited property, allowed to inherit and keep up to £200, and could also keep her own wages and investments.

Because of the 'non-person' status of married women during the Victorian era, it is difficult to understand more clearly the detail relating to the lives of the married female residents of Rock Terrace. After marriage at this time the wives became anonymous, only appearing in the press at the announcement of the births of their children, or their death, or their charitable work. The new Property Act was at least a step in the right direction for the liberation of women.

One of the first new tenants moving into the terrace during this period was Albert Bird and his wife, Sarah. Albert was accountant to the coal merchant, Ellis and Everard, working under Thomas Cooper Goodrich. He had been lodging above a grocery shop at 8 Red Lion Square (now Nelson's, the butchers), but after marrying Sarah, in Bloomsbury, the couple moved into 10 Rock Terrace. When Thomas Goodrich died in 1885, Albert replaced him as manager and moved to 53 High Street (now Neal's Yard Remedies).

Albert was followed into the terrace by Susannah Harris, a fifty-eight-year-old spinster from Little Bytham. She had spent all of her life caring for her farming family but, after her mother died in 1882, at the age of eighty-eight, she was able to move into town, which was also closer to her nephew who farmed at Tinwell. Susannah remained at 10 Rock Terrace until her death in 1901.

During the next few years, two of the most successful brands of today came onto the market. In 1885, Karl Friedrich Benz built the first production car, the Benz Patent Motorwagen, and his company led to the Daimler Benz Corporation. In Atlanta, a pharmacist invented Coca-Cola, currently one of the top three most recognised brands in the world. However, it was the pharmacist's bookkeeper whose distinctive script, of the words Coca-Cola, created its logo, which has never changed.

In England, in 1877, another retiree, Richard Dean Holkings, moved into 4 Rock Terrace with his second wife, Mary Lyon, and their servant Jane Smith. Richard had lived on Scotgate before, in much less agreeable conditions. In 1833, a year after the death of his father, he married Mary Mantle and by 1841 they were living, together with their four children, in a single room in Corporation Buildings. These dwellings were built behind 25 and 26 Scotgate, by Stamford Corporation, in 1796, to house the poor, but living in a slum tenement with poor sanitation was not without risk. Whilst resident there, in the 1840s, Mary and one of her daughters died.

Richard, a tailor, remarried three years after the death of his wife and within a short time his situation had been transformed. By 1849, he had moved to a shop with living quarters in Wellington Lane and then, as a master tailor, was recruiting an apprentice. Obviously successful, Richard was able, by 1851, to move again to larger premises in a very prominent position at the end of Broad Street no. 52, now the Model Fish Bar and restaurant.

53. Holking's shop, c. 1860

54. Model Fish Bar, 2020

For the next twenty-six years Richard ran a clothier's business which specialised in uniforms and ready-made, rather than bespoke, wear. Towards the end of his time at Broad Street, and whilst living at Rock Terrace, Richard devoted time to public service – he became a councillor, a guardian of the Stamford Union, and chairman of the Stamford Temperance Society.

By 1881, one of Richard's daughters, Harriet Haystrat Holkings, had returned to live with her parents in the terrace. She had been a teacher in Newark, and possibly came back to care for her mother, who died in February 1883. Less than a year later Richard embarked upon his third marriage, to Millicent Hall, a widow from Langtoft. Richard, his new wife, and daughter Harriet continued to live at no. 4, with the assistance of a servant, Mary Rudkin, whose surname is still familiar in Stamford. When Richard died in 1892, Harriet stayed on at the terrace for another three years before moving to Rosebery House on Queen Street (no. 45), one of the properties built in the Northfields area after the Enclosure Act of 1871. As a sign that leasing property remained the norm, Harriet later moved from Queen Street to 29 Kings Road, just around the corner, and finally a few doors away to 25 Kings Road, where she died.

In 1886, after he had reached the age of majority, Robert Nicholas Todd-Newcomb travelled to Stamford with his solicitor Thomas Butler, to meet the staff of the *Mercury* and his Stamford tenants. From the outset he decided to leave the *Mercury* to be managed by Thomas, and edited by John Paradise and his deputy, Overbury. Robert had inherited a significant income stream from the *Mercury*, and the Newcomb property portfolio, but remained grounded within his home territory of Cumbria. In 1884, he joined the 1st Volunteer Battalion, King's Own (Royal Lancs. Regiment) as a lieutenant, and remained with this local militia unit until he resigned his commission in 1887. He paid regular visits to Stamford, but these tended to be of a social or charitable nature, such as attending balls at the Assembly Rooms. In his home county he made many charitable gestures with as little fuss as possible, and often only attracting press mention after the event.

On Boxing Day 1886, Stamford was covered in snow and, following complaints by members of the public, many inhabitants were summonsed to appear before the mayor at Stamford petty sessions on 14 January. They had fallen foul of a local by-law stating that 'every occupier of premises shall cause all snow to be removed from the footways adjoining the premises occupied by him before 10 a.m.'. Residents of most of the ten houses in Rock Terrace were amongst those appearing for not clearing the snow on one of the three days after Boxing Day. It was stated that Rock Terrace was particularly bad, and made all the more obvious for some occupiers, because Mrs Kenrick at no. 2 and Mr Taylor at no. 9 had made such a good job of keeping their pavements clear. Nevertheless, the Rock Terrace occupants, Messrs

Bird, Mehew, Holkings and Overbury, together with Miss Harris, all had their charges withdrawn, during what appeared to be a trial to publicly advertise the little known by-law.

55. John Paradise, 1881

When John Paradise died, later in 1887, the *Mercury* printed a handsome tribute to a man who had been personally recruited by Richard Newcomb, almost fifty years earlier. Paradise had given most of his professional life to the *Mercury* and was its editor for nearly forty years, but he was also an important figure within the Stamford community.

He had been a Stamford town councillor for an uninterrupted thirty-three years, a JP for twenty-five years, and mayor of Stamford in 1864. In addition, Paradise was a member of the managing committee of the Stamford and Rutland Infirmary, a governor of the Stamford Endowed Schools, and a trustee of the Stamford Freehold Land Society. During this time he seems to have successfully balanced the liberal views of the *Mercury* with his non-partisan public appointments. The *Mercury* obituary concluded that Paradise had 'exhibited rare talents and singular tact and assiduity, and there can be no doubt that his death deprives the town of an able and energetic administrator'.

Initially, the *Mercury* did not miss a beat with the passing of Paradise, as John Overbury was able to step up immediately. However, Overbury left after only a few years as editor, and the political zeal with which Richard Newcomb and John Paradise had imbued the *Mercury*, began to dissipate, never to return.

CHAPTER 6

The Last Victorian Tenants (1888–1901)

In the late 1880s the terrace remained an attractive proposition for widows, many of whom had made it their home in the past. Between 1888 and 1894, six widows moved in, and one of the first was sixty-eight-year-old Rebecca Southwell at 6 Rock Terrace. Her husband had been a solicitor's managing clerk and together they had thirteen children, including Mary Agnes who married Edward Joyce in 1878, when he was an accountant at the *Mercury*.

The other widows were: Jane Rogers, who had been widowed in 1865, moved into 3 Rock Terrace in 1888, having retired from her draper's shop below the *Mercury* office at 61 High Street; Harriet Pollard (see profile 9), the sister of Thomas Goodrich, moved to no. 1 in 1891; Frances Skrimshire, the widow of the Crown Agent to the Isle of Man, moved into no. 5 in 1892; Mary Ann Sharpe, a farmer's widow, was resident at 7 Rock Terrace from 1893 until her death in 1898; and finally, Susannah Young, the widow of Edward Foster Young, moved into no. 10 in 1894 – who together with Edward had run a large grocery and provisions store at 13 St John's Street, now the site of the Stamford Job Centre.

PROFILE 9

Cared by, Cared for, Cared by

Harriet Helen Pollard   1 Rock Terrace 1891–1902

Like many other tenants, Harriet arrived at Rock Terrace as a widow. She had led a life blighted by family tragedies and ignominy, but could now relax in retirement in the care of her niece.

Harriet was born in Leicester, in 1834, the youngest child of Thomas Goodrich, a wine and spirit merchant operating from Newarke Street, and his wife, Mary Parkinson. Mary's father, Edward, had been a leading member of the Baptist church, licensing his own home in Thurlaston as a Baptist meeting room. It followed that all of their children were baptised in a non-conformist chapel, the Congregational on Bond Street, Leicester.

In 1838, Harriet's father died suddenly of heart disease, leaving her, together with her mother and her older siblings, Edward, Thomas Cooper, Sarah, Charles and Mary, to carve out a new life. Luckily Thomas had made a detailed will, which, after some legal skirmishes with his creditors, provided a safety net for the family. One of his executors was Thomas Ward, a yeoman farmer from Sileby, named in the will as Thomas' father-in-law. In fact, Ward was not strictly his father-in-law, but had taken Mary Parkinson under his wing after her father, Edward, had died, and stepped up again to take Mary and her children into his household.

Two years later there was another blow to the Goodrich family when Edward, the eldest son, died of consumption, aged twenty-two. He had been destined to continue to run his father's wine and spirit business, but the company's assets were then sold. A year later Mary Parkinson Goodrich, aged twelve, died at Ward's house in Sileby. She also died from consumption, possibly due to the transfer of the airborne bacteria of pulmonary tuberculosis from her brother.

Harriet had now witnessed the death of her father and two of her siblings within three years. Gradually, her mother and remaining siblings left Sileby, but having been taken in by Thomas Ward and his wife as a child, Harriet remained with them, as housekeeper, for the rest of their lives. Only after the widowed and blind Thomas died in 1861, at the age of eighty, did Harriet join the rest of her family who had all migrated to Stamford.

In the intervening years Harriet's brother, Thomas Cooper, had become a teacher and a private secretary. He had been well educated at the Wymes-wold Academy and at the newly opened Collegiate School in Leicester where he excelled, winning first prize in French, Latin, and history.

By 1849, the other brother, Charles, was a coal merchant in Stamford, and a few years later Sarah became governess to the Michelson family at 2 St Mary's Place, Stamford, possibly helped by her Baptist connections. She would remain with the Michelson family for the rest of her life, ending as a lady's companion at 1 Broad Street, where she died in 1910.

Charles was successful as a coal agent, became the managing agent for Ellis and Everard and, in 1856, married Mary Turner from Ketton. They lived together at 12 St Mary's Hill, opposite the town hall, and next door to a butcher's shop that had been built above a thirteenth century crypt. The shop was owned by the widowed Mary Pollard who ran the butchery business together with her son John. Early in 1857, Charles and, a then pregnant, Mary, would have witnessed the wedding of Mary's daughter Mercy Pollard to William Hurry, at St Mary's Church, across the road. William had been in the army, was one of the survivors of the six hundred involved in the Charge of the Light Brigade at Balaclava, and was a publican, near Peterborough. However, his arrest for abduction would later cause distress to the family.

56. St Mary's Church, from St Mary's Hill

A few months after the Pollard wedding, Charles' wife, Mary, gave birth to a daughter, Mary Ellen, however, either during or just after the confinement, Mary died. The family rallied around Charles: his mother moved into the house on St Mary's Hill, and his thirty-nine-year-old unmarried brother visited for a time in 1861. By the end of that year, after Thomas Ward's death, Harriet also joined them. It was here that she met John Pollard, the butcher next door, whom she married on 2 August 1862, also at St Mary's Church. By this time, John's mother had retired and moved into 8 Rock Terrace.

Less than a year after their marriage, scandal hit the family as John's brother-in-law, William Hurry, was arrested for abducting a young girl. He remained in gaol for four months awaiting his trial at Cambridgeshire assizes, after which the story broke, and was reported in detail:

> …It appeared that on the 13th of March last, the prisoner, who once kept the Packhorse inn, at Whittlesey, ran away with Martha Burdock, a girl under 16 years of age, and the daughter of John Burdock, of the Dog-in-a-Doublet [an inn that still exists near Thorney]. Hurry obtained a horse and gig from Peterborough, and proceeded to the Great Northern Railway, at Tallington, and booked for Grantham, taking with him a quantity of his wife's wearing apparel....

Apparently, the girl had often been sent by her father to collect tolls nearby, where she seemed to attract the attention of many passing men. William was one such man, but his attraction to the young Martha went too far, and the judge, who, despite the victim blaming tactics of the defence counsel, sentenced him to twelve months hard labour. Bankruptcy followed his imprisonment, but Mercy stuck with him and they moved to London.

In the meantime, apart from John's embarrassment and the concern he may have had for his sister, his time as a butcher was not a success, and, in 1863, John was also made bankrupt. His mother may have helped getting him discharged, but she let the premises to another butcher, and John left the business to become a horsebreaker. Things began to spiral out of control for John. He became involved in some 'larking' at the butcher's shop with a Mr Dodds, and accidentally severed a finger in the process. Then, in August 1864, John was charged and fined twenty-one shillings for an assault on a man with whom he was lodging – a possible indication that he had also become estranged from Harriet. A year later John, aged thirty-two, was dead. He had been admitted to the Stamford Infirmary where he died of 'acute inflammation of the windpipe', which may have been the result of a respiratory infection, or even anaphylactic shock.

With another tragic loss, Harriet was widowed, and now rejoined her family who had moved from St Mary's Hill across the town bridge to 46 High Street, St Martin's, as their housekeeper. It was not long before yet another Goodrich was taken prematurely when, in 1871, Charles died, at the age of forty-four, orphaning his fourteen-year-old daughter. Luckily, family support was again on hand. His ageing mother, Mary, and sister Harriet could care for Mary Ellen at the house, and Thomas Cooper, who had been working as a private secretary in Northumberland, returned immediately, moved into 46 High Street, and took over the coal agency, which his brother had built up.

After her mother died in 1875, Harriet remained as housekeeper to her brother, and guardian to Mary Ellen. Thomas Cooper had by then all but given up his beloved game of cricket. He had in the past played for Leicestershire, and the Gentlemen of Nottinghamshire, and, in 1853, played in a first-class match for the Gentlemen of England versus the Gentlemen of the Marylebone Cricket Club. In 1856, Thomas was also one of the founders of the Free Foresters Cricket Club, which to this day remains the leading wandering club in the country, and can count thirty-three past England captains amongst its past members.

One morning in March 1885, Thomas, who had apparently eaten a hearty breakfast, taken a stroll in his garden, and then enjoyed a cigar, took to his bed and died within two hours. After his death the Free Foresters presented a plaque, which is displayed in St Martin's Church.

Harriet remained in St Martin's for a few more years before moving into 1 Rock Terrace in 1891, where she lived with her niece Mary Ellen, who was working as a coal merchant's clerk. Mary Ellen never married, and spent almost her entire life being cared by, or caring for, her aunt Harriet. When Harriet died, in 1902, Mary Ellen remained at no. 1 until her death in 1928.

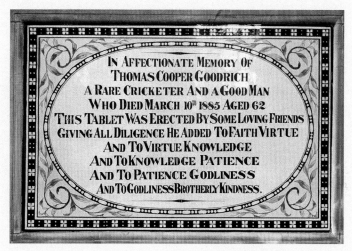

In Affectionate Memory Of
Thomas Cooper Goodrich
A Rare Cricketer And a Good Man
Who Died March 10th 1885 Aged 62
This Tablet Was Erected By Some Loving Friends
Giving All Diligence He Added To Faith Virtue
And To Virtue Knowledge
And To Knowledge Patience
And To Patience Godliness
And To Godliness Brotherly Kindness.

57. Plaque, St Martin's Church

In 1890, Robert Todd-Newcomb, still only twenty-three and an eligible bachelor, set sail for Australia and was away from England for up to nine months. Was this young man of independent means seeking enjoyment or, given that he was not going to be a hands-on proprietor of the *Mercury*, looking for some purpose to his life ahead? On 5 April 1891, Robert was staying at the Bee Hotel in Liverpool, one of only five residents that day. Amongst them was a young French actor, Leon Roche, who was described as a gentleman, living-on-own-means. Robert on the other hand, whilst also a gentleman of wealth, was described as a commercial traveller.

Within six months Robert had struck up a professional relationship with Leon, and had become an impresario. Together they produced a play, *Vida*, which toured England to mixed reviews. This was followed in the spring of 1892 by the more successful *Fourteen Days* – a farce. However, Robert's adventure into showbusiness seems to have ended with this production, and back on home turf he met and married Florence Wright, and settled down to managing his estate and travelling abroad.

After Elizabeth Kenrick and her son had died at 2 Rock Terrace, the house remained vacant for a couple of years, until sisters Elizabeth and Caroline March took up residence in 1892, following the death of their father. These spinster sisters were two of five daughters born to Frederick March, a chemist on the High Street, and Mary Ann Goodwin. After Caroline was born in 1857, her mother died, leaving Frederick with five children all under the age of nine. Luckily, Frederick had the accommodation and financial ability to take on a housekeeper, shop assistant, and servant until such time as his daughters could help in the store and the house. The eldest unmarried daughters became Frederick's housekeeper, stepping into each other's shoes as marriage took some of them away: Emily to a farmer, Mary Harriet to a druggist, and Eliza to a chemist.

By 1881 Elizabeth had become the housekeeper, whilst Caroline was visiting Emily at her farm. Ten years later, Caroline took on the housekeeper duties as Elizabeth had become a schoolmistress. When they moved into the terrace, the two unmarried sisters decided to pool their skills, as housekeeper and teacher, and set up a small preparatory day school, but also took in two or three boarders. It would have provided them with a purpose and a small income, until they moved away in 1897, to retire at St Leonards-on-Sea.

58. Frederick March's chemist shop

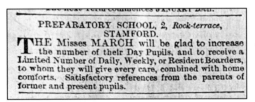

59. Adv. for school, *Mercury* 1 January 1892

Transport within Stamford around the turn of the century remained horse-powered, and like second-hand cars today, there were always dealers to facilitate the buying and selling of the animals. John Clarke was a horse-dealer living at 9 Rock Terrace, and was also an equestrian. In 1896 he was playing polo at Burghley Park and, following a fall, his pony trod on his face and he lost a tooth. Eight years later, at the Burghley Horse Show, Clarke won a trio of first prizes in the polo pony sports gymkhana, including the Postillion Stakes, which involved riding to a post leading another pony, dismounting, changing ponies and riding home.

In 1898, Samuel Fancourt Halliday, the building contractor, became mayor of Stamford for the first time. He had lived in Rock Terrace for a few years in the 1880s, but despite not having children had moved on to larger and more imposing properties. His name lives on in Stamford at Halliday's Yard, previously used as a bus station, but now a multi-purpose commercial site, off Radcliffe Road. His career as a builder in Stamford may have been expected because of the interests of his father, but his life could have taken a very different route (see profile 10).

PROFILE 10

Linen Draper or Builder

Samuel Fancourt Halliday   9 Rock Terrace 1880–1882

In 1851, when six-year-old Samuel went to stay with his aunt, a butcher's wife in Exton, he could not have known that twenty-two years later he would marry his young cousin, Mary Ann, with whom he was playing.

Samuel was born in 1845, the son of Thomas Charity Halliday and Lavinia Fancourt. Thomas was a stonemason and builder, descended from a long line of Halliday masons dating back to the seventeenth century in Rutland, and Lavinia's sister, Mary, had married into the Hibbitt family of Exton. Masonry might have seemed the obvious choice for Samuel's career, but Lavinia may have had thoughts of a more genteel life for her son, based on the success of other Hibbitt brothers- and sisters-in-law who had developed linen draper's businesses in London.

The origin of these businesses was the result of a pregnancy out of wedlock. Maria Hibbitt, the eldest of Lavinia's sisters-in-law, moved to London whilst pregnant, probably to avoid the problems it might have caused for her family. She was joined by Thomas Searson, her cousin and likely father of the child, who was born around 1820. As soon as Thomas reached full age, in 1823, he married Maria and by 1841 Thomas had his own linen draper's business on Camden High Street.

In the years that followed, more of Lavinia's Hibbitt relations migrated to London and became part of a group of linen drapers linked to the Hibbitt family. One, at 51 Leather Lane, was only a ten-minute walk away from where Charles Dickens was living at the time, and the others had prime spots on the High Streets of Camden, Kensington and Marylebone. This success probably influenced Lavinia, and by 1861 Samuel was apprenticed at the Marylebone shop.

Whether due to pressure from his father, a dislike of the linen business or London, or a genetic pull from his ancestry, Samuel forsook his draper's apprenticeship and returned to live with his parents in Greetham. Samuel returned south in 1873 to marry Mary Ann, who was living with her sister Selina in Norwood. Selina's husband was William Gayler, to whom Samuel had been apprenticed, and the success of the drapery business meant that they no longer lived above the Marylebone shop.

Samuel's early training may have helped him develop some people and general management skills, which would be helpful in his father's large group of businesses: building contractors in Greetham and Stamford, farming and corn merchants in Oakham, and quarries in Clipsham. The business became Halliday and Sons around 1870, and in 1874/5 Samuel was involved in the building of Rock Villa (later Rock Lodge) at the bottom of Empingham Road. Thomas Charity, Samuel's father, became a tenant at 9 Rock Terrace in 1878, possibly as a base in Stamford to look after his interests, and in 1880, Samuel and Mary Ann took over from Thomas at no. 9, remaining there for three years.

60. Samuel Halliday, c. 1899

After the death of his father in 1884, Samuel took over, and developed, the Stamford building and contracting business. Samuel moved from Rock Terrace into Rock Villa, and remained there for the rest of his life, other than a short stay at Bredcroft House on Tinwell Road, possibly whilst Rock Villa was being refurbished. In 1892, Samuel became a councillor, and as a mark of the respect he enjoyed within the town, he was elected mayor for three consecutive years: 1898 to 1900.

In London, the Marylebone High Street linen drapers had gone from strength to strength. After William Gayler had completed his apprenticeship at Harvey Nichols, he and Selina had taken over a rat-infested butcher's shop at no. 116, and started a small drapery business. They never closed before eight at night, and in winter the shop was lit by candlelight. As the years passed they expanded by acquiring adjacent premises, and by 1885 were operating at 114–117 Marylebone High Street, as well as two adjoining shops around the corner on South Street (now Blandford Street).

By then, the expanded business had become a department store and was trading as Gayler and Pope, the result of Selina's sister Emily marrying John Pope, a draper's assistant, in 1863. When William Gayler celebrated the store's jubilee in 1907, as chairman of Gayler and Pope, the expansion was complete, and the building stretched the whole block from Blandford Street to St Vincent Street. William died a year later and entrusted his previous apprentice, and brother-in-law, Samuel, to be his executor. Gayler and Pope continued trading until 1966.

As the century neared its end another war began in South Africa. Early fighting against the Boers, using Britain's regular army, led to significant losses, and the decision was taken by the War Office to allow a volunteer force to fight in the war. On 24 December 1899 the Imperial Yeomanry received its Royal Warrant, which stated that the volunteers should be good horsemen and marksmen, and provide their own horses, saddles and clothing. After spending Christmas with his parents at 5 Rock Terrace, Henry Hay set off for Trowbridge where, on 28 December, he became one of the earliest volunteers (see profile 11).

At the same time, in Russia, there was growing unrest amongst the proletariat. With this background, and the recent death of her husband, Elizabeth Grotten decided to return to England, from St Petersburg, and settle with her daughter at 3 Rock Terrace. A year later a newly married couple moved in next door to Elizabeth. Albert Elijah Bassindale, a timber merchant's clerk, had married Alice Carden in December 1890, and, shortly after, made their home at no. 2. In April 1903, their first child, Alice Mary, was born at the house, and by the end of that year they had moved to 49 Queen Street, where another two children, Vera and Tom, were later born.

62. Bassindale family, c. 1914

PROFILE 11

Returned for More

Henry Hay   5 Rock Terrace 1895–1900

Henry Hay was born in Pickford in 1876, the youngest child of ten born to John and Rebecca. Henry's father was a farmer who had retired and moved to Rock Terrace in 1895, after Henry had completed his education at Stamford Grammar School.

Henry was living with his parents when he made the decision to join the Imperial Yeomanry, but he eschewed more local yeomanry groups, instead deciding on the 1st Battalion in Wiltshire, which had precedence over all other battalions in England. He was typical of early recruits who came from the middle and upper classes, and had the added advantage of a good stature for a twenty-three-year-old in 1899 – almost six feet tall and weighing over eleven-and-a-half stone.

At the end of February, after some limited training, Henry and his company paraded through Trowbridge by torchlight, cheered on by the locals, to the train station. They made their way to Liverpool, and on 28 February set sail for the Cape on the SS *Cymric*. After arriving, on 23 March, they marched to Maitland, the location of the base camp. Whilst his comrades marched north into the Orange Free State, it appears that Henry never made it out of the Cape province. His service record shows no sign of sickness or injury, but in June he returned to the UK and remained at HQ until September, when he resigned and returned to Rock Terrace, Stamford. It is unclear why Henry resigned from the yeomanry, however, if he joined up to see some action he may have been disillusioned by being inactive in South Africa for three months.

Within six months everything had changed. Queen Victoria had died, the Boer War was lasting longer than had been anticipated, and there was another drive to recruit volunteers to the Imperial Yeomanry. Henry had also changed. By then weighing fourteen stone, he decided to re-enlist, joining his old 2nd Comp, 1st Batt, in Chippenham on 28 February, and within a month sailed back to South Africa.

The 1st Battalion was operational in the Harrismith area, north of the border of Basutoland (now Lesotho), and Henry was immediately involved in the fighting against the Boer commandos. A lot of the time he was patrolling, escorting, and reconnoitring, but the guerrilla warfare tactics of the Boers meant that he was constantly under threat of ambush, and regularly involved in skirmishes. By October 1891 the constant movement and fighting had taken its toll, and Capt. Sir Charles Fowler of the 1st Battalion wrote that 'the men were in a most deplorable condition, half of them being dismounted and in rags'.

In the spring of 1902, the battalion, under the command of Lieut. Col. Perceval, escorted other troops from the Ladysmith area, past Harrismith, and on to Fouriesberg. By 18 April they were camped nearby, on the Basutoland border, when intelligence arrived that a party of around fifty Boers were holed up in a farm at Moolman's Spruit. The inexperienced and under strength Perceval decided to raid the farm, setting out on the night of 19 April with around a hundred of his battalion (probably including Henry), and around forty

63. Uniform of Imperial Yeomanry, c. 1900

of the South Staffs Mounted Infantry. They rode to within two hundred yards of the farm, dismounted, and then approached with fixed bayonets, but the Boers were expecting them. Capt. Fowler, an old Harrovian baronet, was in the lead group and when he was within twenty yards of the farmhouse he was shot and killed. A battle followed and the Boers, who totalled nearer two hundred, forced Perceval to signal a controlled retreat. Eight of Perceval's attacking force were killed, many injured, and some taken prisoner.

Perceval's scattered troops eventually made it to Fiksburg where they regrouped. By the end of May the war was over and Moolman's Spruit had been its last major conflict. In June, the 1st Battalion, Wiltshire Yeomanry slowly marched south with only occasional problems from the Boers, who were unaware of the end of the war. By the second week of July they had reached Elandsfontein, a staging post and hospital only a hundred miles from Capetown. A couple of weeks later, the officers and over 250 men of the 1st Battalion sailed back to England, but without Henry.

Henry had not travelled the last hundred miles with his comrades, instead opting to resign from the yeomanry at Elandsfontein, in order to join the Natal Police in Pietermariksburg. By then he had earned the Queen's South Africa medal, with three clasps for operations in the Cape, Orange Free State, and Transvaal, as well as the King's South Africa medal, with 1901 and 1902 clasps, for over eighteen months' service during the Boer War.

The decision not to return to England is difficult to understand although, despite the deprivations he had suffered, he may well have fallen for the country. Holt, in his book *The Mounted Police of Natal*, described what the attraction may have been for Henry as 'in times of peace, he has a life which a hard-working man in England would regard as a perpetual holiday on horseback'.

64. Boer war medals

Whilst Henry Hay was at home in Rock Terrace, between tours of duty in South Africa, Queen Victoria had died. The eighty-one-year-old Queen had ruled for over sixty years, and had become ill and frail. At the Isle of Wight, on 22 January 1901, an announcement was posted at the gates of Osborne House informing the world that 'Her Majesty the Queen breathed her last at 6.30pm, surrounded by her children and grand-children'. The Victorian era was over and the United Kingdom looked forward to a new century with a new monarch.

The *Mercury* covered the Queen's death, her obituary, and her funeral in effusive detail, but a month later would have to cover the death of someone personally associated with the newspaper. Robert Todd-Newcomb had just returned from a cruise in South Africa with his wife, Florence, and was staying at the fashionable Hotel Metropole, close to Charing Cross Station. Robert, aged thirty-six, fell ill with a cold virus, which developed into pneumonia and caused his death. His wife, Florence Todd-Newcomb, (see profile 12) inherited Robert's estate, and became the next proprietor of the *Mercury*.

PROFILE 12

The Last of the Newcomb Heirs

Florence 'Zita' Egan-Newcomb Owner, Rock Terrace 1901–1919

By the turn of the nineteenth century Zita, as she had become known, was at ease with the highest level of London society and on the evening of 15 May 1903 was presented to the Queen consort, Alexandra of Denmark, at Buckingham Palace, by Mrs Walpole Heron-Maxwell. Zita was not of aristocratic stock, and this was far removed from her early life.

Florence Wright was born in Aston, Warwickshire, in 1872, the fifth child of Henry Fox Wright and his wife, Emily Henrietta Edwards. Henry was landlord of the Castle and Falcon Hotel in Dudley, and at the same time worked as a commercial traveller for Thomas Willis, a tea, grocery and hop wholesaler. In 1869, Henry took advantage of his employer of over sixteen years, and was caught and charged with embezzlement. The case was heard by the Earl of Dudley, and Henry, who was found guilty of taking £71, was sentenced to eighteen months hard labour.

In 1871, Henry, having completed his sentence, was still living in the Midlands and working as a commercial traveller, but after Florence was born he moved his family to Barrow-in-Furness. There he set up an oil and varnish manufacturing business which seems, initially, to have been successful, enabling the family to live in the six-bedroom Roozebrook House at Aldingham. During this time, he became a local Freemason and was active in the community. However, in 1883 the business collapsed with major debts, and once again Henry became bankrupt.

The family moved to a smaller house in Barrow, and Henry, without any inherited wealth and with a return to his precarious commercial traveller occupation, still managed to provide a middle-class existence for his family, in a comfortable home with a live-in servant. Florence had witnessed the highs and lows of living in this remote part of England, and in the next decade she would blossom into an incredibly beautiful young lady with an independent spirit.

During this time, Florence met Robert Todd-Newcomb, who had inherited the *Mercury* and the Newcomb estate assets when he was two years old. Robert was the son of a yeoman farmer, who had died prematurely, and lived with his mother at 'The Guards' in nearby Kirkby Ireleth, their family home for four generations. In 1893, Florence, wearing 'a handsome white satin Duchess costume with court train' married Robert, followed by a wedding breakfast at her father's house in Barrow.

Robert was, by accounts, a slightly shy, humble man given to anonymous charitable gestures. He visited Stamford regularly, but was never involved in the day-to-day management of the *Mercury*. Together with Florence they set up home at Bankfield Hall, in Urswick, and also travelled extensively. After one of their many trips, a cruise to South Africa, Robert became ill and died on 24 February 1901.

Robert's death, at the age of thirty-six, meant that Florence inherited the whole of his estate, worth over £10 million at today's value. The newly widowed Florence appointed her brother to manage the *Mercury*, started to hedonistically enjoy the fruits of the Newcomb estate, and became known as 'Zita'. Although her centre of 'social' gravity moved almost entirely to London, where she lived on Park Lane, Zita did maintain Bankfield House, where she ran a stud farm. She was a strong and determined woman and, in addition to her interest in horses and horsemanship, she pursued her passion for racing: her Richard-Brasier and Daimler motorcars winning races in 1905, at average speeds of over twelve miles-per-hour.

65. Zita with motor racing trophies, c. 1905

From about 1903, Zita had the unusual misfortune of being stalked by a man who had become besotted with her. James Craik had bombarded her with letters, and called at, and even broken into, her apartment since meeting her at a reception. This situation came to a head in November 1905, when he was arrested for threatening to kill Zita's solicitor and her friend Victor Egan.

On 30 January 1906, Zita remarried at the society church of St George's in Hanover Square, London. Her new bridegroom was Victor Augustus Seymour Egan, the grandson of Cornelius Egan, of Bulloch Castle, near Dublin, and the friend who had defended her against the attractions of Craik. Showing her determination and strength of character, Zita insisted from the outset that Victor should have no part in the running of the *Mercury*, nor in the management of her affairs. This was a wise move given Egan's past, and what was to follow. Probably unknown to Zita, Victor Egan had been prosecuted in 1893 when he and a friend had been pretending to be brothers, using alias names, and indulged in some petty theft. The eighteen-year-old Victor apparently had a circle of respectable friends, but this escapade had led to two weeks on remand in Holloway gaol whilst awaiting his court appearance.

Zita also had to broach the issue of maintaining the Newcomb name as stipulated in Robert Newcomb's will, written almost forty years earlier. Victor Egan may have refused to change his name, and indeed their future children were to be christened solely with the surname Egan. However, although Victor Egan did not change his name legally, the couple were known as the Egan-Newcombs, and when Victor Egan was adjudicated as bankrupt, in 1915, it was as Victor Egan-Newcomb.

Although James Craik had been sent away to South Africa by his family and friends, with the aim of halting his infatuation with Zita, on his return he persisted with his unwanted attention. In March 1906 he was committed to an asylum, from which he escaped, and in November he again broke into the Park Lane apartment where Zita and Victor lived with a butler, housemaid and cook. A fight ensued, Zita was assaulted, and Craik bit and attempted to strangle Victor. The attack was widely reported in the press and the case was heard at the Old Bailey, at which Craik was found guilty, but insane, and sentenced to be detained at His Majesty's pleasure at Banstead asylum.

By August 1911, Victor and Zita had two young boys and had moved to 3 Rutland Gate. Here, Zita must have been horrified when approached and kissed by James Craik who, only a few days earlier, had been released from the asylum on the orders of the Home Secretary, Winston Churchill. James was again arrested, brought before the court and, with Zita appearing as a witness, was remanded. At the end of the case James rushed towards Zita, who screamed and jumped up to the bench whilst six officers detained him. The case was again widely reported, with much criticism directed towards Churchill for releasing the prisoner, against the advice of the asylum medical officer. Craik was sent back to Banstead, and later transferred to Broadmoor. He died in 1961 at the age of eighty-three.

Victor and Zita's third child was born in 1912, and soon after Zita's financial situation began to deteriorate. Her main income from the *Mercury* had dried up, as its circulation, which had halved from its high at the turn of the century to 1912, had halved again by 1919. Victor's bankruptcy in 1915 and Zita's costly lifestyle, including the children's education at Sunningdale Preparatory School, all contributed, which led Zita to take decisive action. In October 1919, she liquidated almost all of the Newcomb estate property assets, save the *Mercury*, in what amounted to a fire sale. At the same time Zita sold the

66. Zita c. 1918

London family home at 3 Rutland Gate, and it would seem that Victor and Zita then lived apart.

The Egan-Newcombs had three boys, but their marriage deteriorated and eventually ended in divorce, brought by Zita in December 1922, and in their legal surname of Egan. The timing of the divorce was important as it preceded the Matrimonial Causes Act of 1923, which made divorce by a woman somewhat easier. In 1922, Zita not only had to prove adultery, but also another serious cause which could include cruelty, desertion and/or rape. In her petition Zita cited numerous acts of cruelty, desertion for at least two years, and multiple acts of adultery with 'some woman'. Although classed as perjury it was not uncommon for divorce to be agreed between the parties, despite affidavits being sworn stating that no collusion had taken place. In this case the divorce file points towards a truly contested petition, with Victor initially refuting all accusations, and Zita providing corroborating witness statements. After the desertion and adultery, but not the cruelty, were accepted by the court, the decree nisi was granted in December 1923, and Zita was awarded costs and the custody of her three boys.

In 1929, Zita finally sold the *Mercury*, bringing to an end an almost 150-year relationship between the Newcomb name and this regional newspaper. At the same time, she splashed out on a gift for her three boys. Zita purchased the *Hispania*, a gaff cutter racing yacht, built for HRH Don Alfonso VIII, the King of Spain. The eldest son, Patrick, who was only twenty-two at the time, took control of the *Hispania* and regularly raced her during Cowes week. A few years later his younger, naval lieutenant brother, Rupert, joined him and they became regulars at Cowes until the war, when yachting was abandoned.

In 1934, ten years after his divorce, Victor became the fourth husband of Elsie Ferguson, the beautiful fifty-one-year-old American stage and film actress. They spent their married life between their farm in Connecticut and villa in Cap d'Antibes, until Victor died in 1956.

Zita spent the rest of her life living in an apartment on Curzon Street in London, and died in March 1940 leaving an estate of just under £2 million at today's value. This publican's daughter had, through the premature deaths of a farmer and his son, unexpectedly inherited the Newcomb estate, and used this wealth to her advantage. She led an extravagant lifestyle, became accepted by London society and, through these new-found connections, secured a place for her sons at Eton College.

CHAPTER 7

Tenants During the Great War (1902–1918)

The new proprietor of the *Mercury* would, as her husband before her, have little to do with the day-to-day management of the newspaper. Her brother Henry Fox Wright, who lived in Sleaford, took over from Thomas Butler as the owner's representative, William Poole remained editor and Edward Joyce remained the day-to-day manager.

In the terrace the make-up of the tenants was also changing as, by 1902, more than half of the houses were occupied by wage earners. Most of the tenants could no longer afford servants, whose wages had increased considerably, some took in lodgers and others had assistance from charities. John Hay, for example, at 5 Rock Terrace, was granted an award in 1904 by the Royal Agricultural Benevolent Institution, as he found himself in financial difficulty. Also, despite being introduced in 1902, many in the terrace could not afford the luxury of electricity, and some would remain without it until the 1960s.

One of the new tenants during this period was James Fuller Scholes, a retired horse-drawn cab proprietor (see profile 13). He moved into 4 Rock Terrace in 1903 with his wife, Annie, and when she died at the house in 1907 he moved out of the terrace. Also moving out, to live with their son William in Little Haywood, Staffordshire, was John Hay and his wife, who lived next door. A bank clerk, Herbert Small, took the place of Scholes, and William King, the retired manager of The George Hotel, took over no. 5 from Hay.

PROFILE 13

Last Surviving Witness of the Stamford Bull Run

James Fuller Scholes   4 Rock Terrace 1903–1907

In November 1838, four-year-old James watched from an upstairs window of his parents' house, the Chequers Inn at 27 St Peter's Street, as a noisy mob chased a bull along the road towards Rutland Terrace. At the end of the street two wagons blocked the bull's path, forcing it to turn, run back towards town and down to the meadows. The following year the Stamford Bull Run, which had taken place for over seven centuries, was finally brought to an end.

67. Chequers Inn

Following the death of James' father in 1841 and his aunt in 1845, his widowed mother and uncle, Thomas, married. Thomas had been a publican, running the Blue Bell at Asfordby, and together they continued to run the Chequers Inn for over twenty-five years. During the 1870s they retired to 5 Eight Acres, a lane which runs from Rock Road to Foundry Road, where James was to develop his livery stable business.

James, from a researcher's point of view, disappeared from the genealogical radar after 1841 and did not resurface until the census of 1861 when he was lodging in Lincoln and working as a millwright. In the intervening years it is assumed that he moved away from Stamford to be apprenticed to a millwright and learn his trade. A few years later he married Ann James from Washingborough, only four miles from Lincoln.

James returned to Stamford and by 1871 was living at 9 St Peter's Street, the same street in which he had lived as a child and where his mother was still an innkeeper. In the meantime, he had acquired some eclectic business interests as, in the local 1872 directory, he is listed as a millwright, brass-founder, corn and flour dealer, and horse and carriage letter. After another decade James had whittled down his businesses and concentrated on running a livery yard and equine cab business from 20 Foundry Road, where he also lived with his wife and two boys, James William and Clarence Charles Edwin.

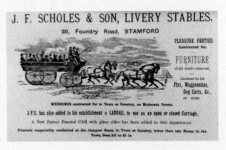

68. Adv. for Scholes livery

James' mother, Mary Ann, died in 1890 at the age of ninety – perhaps a genetic indicator of James' future longevity. In the mid-1890s James retired, and he and Annie moved to 'a small house with great character', 3 Barn Hill (now used as an annex to the Crown Hotel), and James William, who had been working for his father as a groom, became an ostler at The George Hotel.

After a spell at Barn Hill, James and Annie moved into 4 Rock Terrace, where Annie died in 1907. It was a difficult time for the family as within three years both of James' daughters-in-law had also died, leaving his sons as widowers in their early forties. James William, who had been living in London, returned to Stamford and, together with Clarence, resided in Pretoria Cottage on Foundry Road.

After Annie's death, James moved out of Rock Terrace into a smaller terraced property, 24 St Peter's Street, again back to the street where he was born, and where he would die in 1929. Both James William and Clarence remarried, in 1913 and 1914 respectively, and Clarence moved to 21a St Peter's Street, a few doors away from his ageing father.

In the same year, the famous son of Stamford, Malcolm Sargent, took a step that would lead to his musical education, and a successful career. He was attending Bluecoat School (then a preparatory school for Stamford Grammar), and was recommended, and accepted for, one of the six scholarships to the senior school. His father was organist at St John's Church, and, from an early age, Malcolm displayed a prodigious talent, sailing through piano examinations under the tutelage of Mrs Tinkler, in Broad Street.

In 1908, Minnie Wright, the widow of Horace Wright, moved into 2 Rock Terrace. Minnie had been living with her husband at 31 St Paul's Street, but, at the beginning of 1908, he died. Horace had been a master baker and confectioner at 8 All Saint's Place, and in 1873 was mayor of Stamford. After retiring from his bakery business he became a rate collector. Minnie did not inherit enough to be a lady of independent means and to provide an income she took in lodgers at no. 2, as well as running the Stamford Registry, an employment agency providing domestic staff.

ALL Classes of Servants wanted at Mrs. Wright's Stamford Registry (late Balderston), 2, Rock-terrace, Stamford. Cooks, £20-£22; Nurse for Stamford, £18; Parlourmaids, £12-£16; Upper Housemaids, £20-£22; Cook-Generals, £14-£16; Generals and Kitchenmaids, £10-14. No engagement no fee.

69. Adv. for the Registry, *Mercury* 21 August 1908

Horace's death coincided with the passing of the Old Age Pensions Act, which provided a maximum state pension of five shillings per week. Minnie would not have qualified for this as it was only available to those earning less than £21 per annum, and that was equivalent to the rent Minnie was paying for Rock Terrace at the time.

In May 1910, King Edward VII died and was succeeded by George V. He had been an inveterate smoker of cigarettes and cigars, and suffered an extended bout of bronchitis, followed by several heart attacks. At a memorial service for the late King at St John's Church in Stamford, Malcolm Sargent concluded with a rendition of Chopin's funeral march. Later that year Albert Hayes, of the coachbuilding company, died, pre-deceasing his father John who lived for another six years.

The mix of other tenants at this time included an engineer, piano tuner, grocer, and bricklayer, as well as the widows Goodrich and Grotten (see profile 14), and the editor of the *Mercury*. In 1911 they were joined by Cecil Cunnington, (see profile 15) a telegraphist working at the post office, who would only have a few years left of the Belle Époque, before serving in WWI. He would be joined, in war service, by the Lenton brothers from 5 Rock Terrace, and although other tenants did not fight, the families of past, present and future tenants would suffer losses during the conflict.

70. Rock Terrace/ Scotgate

That year the authorities changed the postal addresses of the terrace. Instead of 1 to 10 Rock Terrace the houses became 32 to 41 Scotgate. The Rock Terrace addresses were not reinstated until after WWII but to avoid confusion for the reader they remain a constant in this history.

PROFILE 14

The Burrows Ladies of Greatford

Jane Burrows	6 Rock Terrace	1844–1848
	5 Rock Terrace	1849–1856
Elizabeth Grotten (née Burrows)	3 Rock Terrace	1900–1924
Charlotte Lenton (née Burrows)	5 Rock Terrace	1914–1931
Fanny Burrows	3 Rock Terrace	1900–1935
	9 Rock Terrace	1936–1939

Whilst researching the tenants of Rock Terrace, one name, Burrows, appeared multiple times. Whilst not a particularly unusual name, the fact that they were all related to Lancelot Burrows, a gardener from Greatford, was unexpected.

Jane was Lancelot's younger sister, and had spent most of her young life in service, when in 1844, at the age of thirty-nine, she became one of the first maids to live in the terrace. Jane had come to work for her new mistress, Charlotte Twopenny, and remained with her for over thirty-five years. In 1848, she helped Charlotte move from no. 6 to no. 5, and when Charlotte moved away from Stamford, to support her widowed brother in Devon, Jane was retained as their maid and cook. When Jane returned to Stamford, after Charlotte's death, she moved in with her niece Sarah Jane, one of Lancelot's daughters. Sarah Jane had married a master butcher who died in 1879, leaving Sarah to continue as a butcher with the help of her children and their staff. The butcher's shop, and accommodation above, was at 11 All Saints' Place, which remained a butcher's shop until the 1990s, after which it became a restaurant, currently Hoppi Dorri.

Sarah died in the last quarter of 1882 as did Jane, aged seventy-seven, at the home of her nephew, a baker in Horncastle. It was almost another fifty years, after Jane left, before another Burrows moved into the terrace, and this time it was as a mistress, rather than a maid. Lancelot's daughter Elizabeth had returned to England as a widow and moved into 3 Rock Terrace in 1900, together with her daughter Constance-Emilie, and Fanny her youngest sister. Elizabeth Burrows was born in Greatford, in 1838, and it appears that she was not sent out as a teenager to be a servant girl, as in 1861 she was visiting her brother, a baker, in London.

Within two years of that visit to the metropolis, Elizabeth met and married Vasiliy Alexandrovich Grotten, the son of a Russian merchant from St Petersburg. Vasiliy, or William as he was known in England, was, in 1861, working as a cotton merchant's clerk in Liverpool, probably as part of his training before joining his father's merchant house. The couple were married in Stamford and then settled in Tranmere, just across the Mersey from Liverpool, where William continued to work, and where England's major cotton exchange was located. In 1865, Elizabeth gave birth to Constance-Emilie who was baptised in Tranmere in 1867.

A few years later the family moved to St Petersburg where William joined his father's business, which had been trading since 1798. In 1878, possibly after his father's death, William's career took a different course. He became a stockbroker, and the family lived a comfortable life in an apartment, 16 Makarova, on the embankment of the Little Neva River, (ground floor entrance below the dome of Ekaterininskaya church). This was a far cry from the workman's cottage Elizabeth had left in Greatford. The property was built in 1823, for Savva Yakovlev, a merchant, and the architect was A I Melnikov, who was responsible for many churches and

public buildings across Russia. The yellow-ochre building on the Makarova Embankment was designed to have shops on the ground floor, warehouses and offices on the first floor, and residential apartments on the second floor. It is now one of the many cultural heritage buildings in St Petersburg.

71. Makarova Embankment

William probably died in 1899, as 1900 is the last date he is included in the local directory. At the same time anti-establishment unrest was simmering in St Petersburg, and Elizabeth and Constance-Emilie returned to England. The timing was fortunate as in January 1905 unarmed citizens in St Petersburg marched on the Winter Palace to present a petition to Czar Nicholas II. Unfortunately, the Imperial Guard opened fire on the protesters, resulting in death and injury. This was dubbed Bloody Sunday and led to the 1905 St Petersburg Revolution which, it is said, in turn led to the 1917 Russian Revolution, after which the Imperial family was assassinated. Elizabeth and Constance-Emilie lived together in Rock Terrace for the rest of their lives and were outlived by Fanny.

Fanny was another of Lancelot's daughters who did not leave home as a child to live as a maid-of-all-work. Instead, she remained at Greatford, looking after her family until Lancelot died in 1877, after which she moved with her mother, Ann, to 8 Adelaide Street, where they remained until her mother's death in January 1900. Fanny was named as her mother's sole executor, which suggests that Ann, who had not seen Elizabeth for almost twenty years, may have died before her daughter's return from St Petersburg.

For a few years until her marriage in 1883, Charlotte, another of Lancelot's daughters, also lived at Adelaide Street with her mother and sister. Charlotte was born in 1849, in Greatford, and as no record can be found of her in the 1871 Census there is a possibility that she travelled with her sister to St Petersburg in order to help with the young Constance-Emilie. This may be a fancible idea but getting to St Petersburg by packet steamer from Hull in five days or by train from London in six was, in 1870, not as difficult as one might imagine.

If Charlotte did travel to St Petersburg, she was back in Stamford before 1881 and working as an assistant bootmaker. It was through this work that she met Harry Samuel Lenton, who was the manager of Henry Cooper's shoe shop at 18 High Street, and in 1882 they were married. A year later Cooper retired; Harry took over the business, and moved himself and Charlotte into the accommodation above the shop. He immediately made the business his own, with a sale of Cooper's old stock, and, for the next thirty years, it continued as a successful enterprise. Five children were born above the shop (now a Seasalt clothing outlet) between 1886 and 1890, and when it was time for Harry to retire, in 1914, two had flown the nest. In 1914, the Lenton family moved into 5 Rock Terrace, but the onset of war heralded a terrible period of parental concern as all three of their sons were to see action.

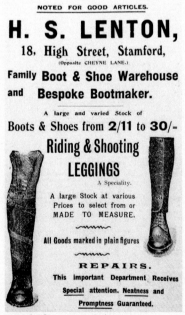

72. Adv. for Lenton's boots

For ten years, after Charlotte moved into No 5, the three Burrows sisters were together in the terrace separated by only one house. They were there for each other to celebrate their successes and mourn their losses. One by one they passed on, Elizabeth and Harry in 1924, Charlotte in

1931, and Constance-Emilie in 1935. Now alone, and aged seventy-nine, Fanny was taken in by the Marjoram family at no. 9, and died in 1942.

In the first one hundred years of Rock Terrace the three Burrows sisters, and their aunt Jane, had spent a combined ninety-two years living there, between 1844, when Richard Newcomb was still alive, to the outbreak of WWII, ninety-five years later.

Malcolm Sargent had not been given an entirely easy ride by the fee-paying boarders at Stamford Grammar, who looked down on the day-boy with a scholarship. However, he was immersed in his music, particularly the organ, and was taking additional instruction from Percy Murrell, Stamford's leading organist at All Saints' Church, who moved into 7 Rock Terrace in 1914. Malcolm left the grammar school in 1910, having passed the matriculation for an external music degree from Durham University. For the next four years he lived at home, studying, practising, and playing. During this time, he became, aged sixteen, an Associate of the Royal College of Organists, and in 1914 received his Bachelor of Music degree from Durham. In the same year he was one of over 100 to apply for the position of organist at Melton Mowbray parish church. Despite being the youngest, he succeeded and his illustrious professional career took off.

The build up to WWI had been slow, but in the first few days of August 1914 the pace dramatically accelerated. Germany declared war on Russia on 1 August and, two days later, on France. Britain had signed treaties with both France and Russia, in 1904 and 1907 respectively, so must have been contemplating their involvement, but the final straw was Germany's invasion of neutral Belgium, on the morning of 4 August. Belgium immediately asked for Britain's assistance, having also signed a treaty in 1839, and by that evening Britain declared that she was in a state of war with Germany. Almost immediately, if they had not already done so, manufacturing companies in Stamford focussed on supporting the war effort: Blackstone & Co made shell casings; Kitson Empire Lighting Company, torpedo heads; and Hayes & Son, ammunition carts and stretchers.

From that moment the horrors of the Great War unfolded, and over the following weeks, months, and years, families with connections to Rock Terrace were involved as they endured the weekly listings in the *Mercury* of the maimed, missing and dead, and waited anxiously for the postman to bring good news, and bad.

On the 28 August 1914, thirty-seven men from Stamford joined the 4th Lincolnshire Regiment. No recruiting officer had been present in Stamford, so the boys, after a rousing send-off in the town, were driven in motor vehicles to Luton, to sign their attestation forms. Amongst them was Charles Goodeve Bird, the son of Albert who had lived at 10 Rock Terrace in the 1880s, John Frewin Lenton, whose parents had just moved into no. 5, and Cyril Hensman Joyce, whose brother Clifford lived at no. 9.

On 1 March 1915, after some training, they sailed to France, together with William Richardson Wright, who had joined the 4th Lincs. through another route. William, like Charles Bird, was an alumnus of Stamford Grammar School, and had lived at 2 Rock Terrace with his mother, Minnie. Throughout the summer they were based in an area south of Ypres, defending a position near the Messines Ridge. By October they had moved south towards Loos with 138th Brigade, of the 46th Division, which was planning an advance on the Hohenzollern Redoubt, an area of higher ground held by the Germans.

What followed, on 13 October, was a scene written about, and caricaturised, many times, but which, in this instance, is taken from eye-witness accounts. Charles and John, like other infantrymen, huddled in an advanced trench, taken earlier from the Germans and strewn with their bodies. Their bayonets were fixed, and, as the hour of attack approached, they nervously looked at their watches as the parapet ladders were put in place. The whistle blew at 2 p.m., and the three boys, who were in the first wave with the 138th Brigade, went over the top, heading for the west face of the redoubt, 200 yards away. During the next ten minutes it was carnage, and even though the west face was taken, the plan to take the wider area failed. In those few insane minutes almost four hundred officers and men of the 4th Lincs. were either killed, wounded or missing. Amongst those killed were Charles and John. Of the thirty-seven Stamford men who joined the 4th Lincs. on 28 August, eight were killed and a further five injured in the attack. Across all brigades involved in the battle, there were over 3,500 casualties, and the later official history of WWI stated that, 'The fighting on the 13th–14th October had not improved the general situation in any way and had brought nothing but useless slaughter of infantry'.

For Harry and Charlotte Lenton, at 5 Rock Terrace, the situation took a cruel twist, as many of those killed were initially posted as missing in action, and it may have been a long wait before any confirmation of John being killed in action was received. But they also had two other sons in the army. Frederick joined the Royal Engineers in November 1914, and sailed to the Dardanelles in July 1915. During the war he was commissioned as temporary second lieutenant, and in June 1918 he was mentioned in despatches and awarded the Military Cross for conspicuous gallantry and devotion to duty as 'He took charge of the whole of the lines and circuit arrangements for a composite force, and thanks to his extreme zeal, energy, and fine example, his men carried out their duties under very trying conditions in a most efficient manner'.

Their other son, Harry Lancelot, was married and living in Camberwell when he joined the Royal Garrison Artillery in December 1915. Harry did not see action, as a signaller, until May 1918, when he was involved in the attack on the Drocourt–Quéant line, near Cambrai, which precipitated the German retreat. On 1 November, Harry fell whilst mending a telephone cable and injured his knee, requiring him to be evacuated to England before the armistice on 11 November. After his recovery, he spent the remainder of his service with 11 Fire Command at Dover.

William Richardson Wright had been a territorial with the Lincolnshire Regiment, and when war was declared he returned from his work in London and joined the 4th Lincs. He survived the attack on the Hohenzollern Redoubt, was later promoted to sergeant, and, in 1916, was commissioned in the field as a second lieutenant. In April that year he was on the front line, near Mont St Eloi, when a German mine exploded just in front of his trench. William, who was buried under eight feet of earth and detritus, was killed, along with fifteen of his men. His body was never recovered.

Cyril Hensman Joyce also survived the ill-fated attack on the redoubt, and went on to be awarded the Military Cross in May 1918. Sydney, the brother of Charles Goodeve Bird, had emigrated to Canada, but joined the Royal Canadian Engineers, a militia group, and travelled to France to support the British war effort. Horace, the brother of William Wright, who had been living in London, joined the Honourable Artillery Company.

73. Stamford War Memorial

Finally, one other Stamfordian linked to the terrace was Frederick Reginald Paradise Dickinson, the son of a chemist who rented his shop from the Newcomb heirs. Frederick's grandfather had married Agnes, one of the daughters of John Paradise, and his widowed mother, Eunice, moved into 2 Rock Terrace in 1921. Frederick Reginald, wanting to follow in his father's footsteps, was apprenticed to Arthur Weddell, a chemist in Colchester, who was born at 6 Rock Terrace in 1852 and had been apprenticed in Stamford. As Frederick was living in Essex at the time of the declaration of war, he joined the 7th Essex Regiment and was quickly commissioned as a second lieutenant, possibly due to his time with the Lincolnshire Yeomanry. He became attached to the 5th East Kent Regiment, and in February 1916 was shipped to Mesopotamia. There he contracted paratyphoid and had to be invalided back to England to recover. His later postings are unknown, but, in July 1917, he was promoted to lieutenant. After the war he did not return to a career as a chemist, instead becoming a commercial traveller, living at 2 Blomfield Mansions, Shepherds Bush.

This sample of fighting men, linked to the ten houses of Rock Terrace, provides a microcosm of the grief and worry that was also seen across Stamford, and indeed throughout the United Kingdom. It is hard to imagine these stories multiplied far and wide, but sadly, much easier to understand the number of three million British men killed or wounded during WWI.

PROFILE 15

Success from Adversity

Cecil Herbert Cunnington   4 Rock Terrace, 1911–1917

From the moment of his father's premature death, Cecil's life was never going to be straightforward.

His father, Thomas Fisher Cunnington, had been in service to the Earls of Crawford at Haigh Hall in Cheshire, starting as a footman and rising to become an under-butler. He met his future wife, Elizabeth, at the hall where she was a kitchen maid, and their busiest and probably most exciting time at Haigh was in June 1873 when Lord and Lady Crawford hosted a three-day visit of the Prince and Princess of Wales.

A few months later Thomas and Elizabeth married in Mayfair, London, possibly whilst working at the Earl's London residence at 9 Grosvenor Square. Children followed the marriage: Thomas Fisher, was born in 1874; Henry Philip in 1876; Elizabeth Georgiana in 1878; and finally, in 1883, Cecil Herbert.

The 25th Earl of Crawford died in 1880, and this may have precipitated Thomas' move from Haigh Hall to Eaton Hall, the seat of Hugh Grosvenor, the 1st Duke of Westminster. It was a straightforward career move on Thomas' part, as he became butler to the wealthiest commoner in the land. It was at Eaton that Cecil was born, and where, on 2 December 1884, his father died of 'disease of valves of heart'. Following Thomas' death, Elizabeth fell into a state of severe depression, and in January 1886 the police found her wandering the streets of Chester in a parlous state. Following an assessment, Elizabeth was committed to the Cheshire County Lunatic Asylum where she remained, without respite from her 'melancholia', until her death in 1908, also from vascular disease. At the same time, Georgiana and Cecil, aged eight and three, were admitted to the Cheshire workhouse.

It seems that, almost immediately, the Duke of Westminster came to the rescue. The two eldest boys, Thomas and Philip, were placed in an industrial school for destitute boys, on board the converted HMS *Clio*, moored in the Menai Strait. The school had been set up by a charity, of which the Duke was president. Georgiana and Cecil were removed from the workhouse and sent to East Grinstead. There, Georgiana became a scholar at St Margaret's Orphanage School for Girls, and Cecil, who as a boy could not join his sister, was fostered to a nearby family who took in the young brothers of girls at the orphanage.

After the Duke had set the children on a path that avoided the workhouse, various sisters of the children's late father became involved in their welfare. Thomas, the eldest son, had become a merchant seaman after leaving HMS *Clio*, and spent some time with his aunt Sarah Jane in Derby. In 1892, with the ubiquitous anchor tattoo on his arm, Thomas joined the Royal Navy, but in 1895 his career came to a tragic end. Able Seaman Cunnington was in a party of seventy-one who set off from HMS *Edgar* in its eighteen-oared fully rigged pinnace for some small arms training on an island in the bay off of Chemulpo (now Incheon), South Korea. Whilst there, the weather dramatically deteriorated, and on return to the mother ship the crew battled against the swell and the lashing wind. As soon as the sail was raised the boat was overcome and quickly sank, and forty-eight sailors, including Thomas, succumbed to the turbulent waters.

Philip, after leaving HMS *Clio*, remained in Lancashire and spent the rest of his life working for the Mersey Dock Board and rising to the position of dock master. Georgiana would have left St Margaret's as a sixteen- or seventeen-year-old and gone into service, for which she had been trained. Cecil would have left his foster home at the time that Georgiana had left the orphanage, and moved to Exton, his late father's birthplace, where he lived with his spinster aunts, Caroline and Annie, who ran the local post office.

At Exton, Cecil attended the local school, the church Sunday school and witnessed life in a post office. His aunt Caroline, who was the postmistress, was probably instrumental in helping Cecil into his first job, as in 1899 the sixteen-year-old Cecil became a telegram boy at the Oakham Post Office, and moved into lodgings nearby. Cecil remained in the employment of the General Post Office (GPO) for the rest of his working life.

In 1905, he married Kate Atton from Braunstone, and their first child, who unfortunately died within a year, followed in 1906. Cecil was transferred to the Stamford Post Office in 1907, and a year later his son Reginald was born and probably baptised at St John's Church, where Cecil was in the choir, and Malcolm Sargent's father was the organist. Now settled in Stamford, and working as a sorting clerk and telegraphist, Cecil and his family were able, in 1910, to move into 4 Rock Terrace. At the same time, Arthur Chamberlin from Norfolk moved to the Stamford Post Office, and worked alongside Cecil in a similar position.

74. Cecil Cunninngton c. 1914

When Britain declared war on Germany in August 1914, Arthur and Cecil quickly volunteered. Telegraphists were in great demand for field support, and both men signed up for signals companies in the Royal Engineers. Just before Cecil left the post office for the army he was promoted to supervising clerk: a position to which he would return after the war.

Cecil trained at Newark with the 11th Division, and Arthur in Chatham with the 17th Division. On 12 June 1915, Cecil's division received notice to prepare to sail from Liverpool to Gallipoli at the end of that month. Meanwhile, Arthur was informed that his division would join the British Expeditionary Force (BEF) on the Western Front early in July. Both men leaving for active duty around the same time may have been a coincidence that led to the dramatic consequences that followed.

Arthur may have been having an affair with Cecil's wife prior to joining up, but was certainly with her around the middle of June, before departing for the front. It is also possible that Cecil returned home en route to Liverpool, and either found them together or discovered the affair at that time. Cecil departed for Gallipoli in the knowledge that he had been cuckolded by Kate, and did not return to the UK for a couple of years, during which time he saw action in the Dardanelles, at Suez, and at the battles of the Somme and Ypres.

During his time away, Cecil received a letter from Kate saying, 'I think it is quite time I made my intentions known to you with regards to what I intend doing after the war. I shall not return to live with you as your wife, because I have already spent a week-end with A.W. Chamberlin, and he also visited me at Rock Terrace. You can take what action you think in this matter'. When Cecil returned on leave towards the end of 1917, he immediately filed for divorce and the custody of his son. On 19 November, the High Court ordered 'that a sealed copy of the petition filed in this case be sent by registered post addressed to 17th Signalling Company, Royal Engineers 17th Division, BEF France'. This copy was for Arthur, the co-respondent, who it was alleged had committed adultery 'on or about the fourteenth day of June 1915 at 4 Rock Terrace'. Neither Kate nor Arthur contested the petition.

75. Divorce file, 1918

76. Memorial at Stamford PO

On 7 June 1918, Justice McCardie granted Cecil the decree nisi, custody of his son and costs. The following day Arthur was killed in action near Acheux, France, and the court, unaware of his death, sent the order for him to pay sixty pounds, eleven shillings and threepence in costs. It is apparent from Kate's letter that Arthur and Kate were committed to each other, and this was confirmed as Arthur had informed the army that all of his field possessions should be sent to her. Kate was also named as the sole beneficiary in Arthur's will.

Cecil returned to the UK and was demobbed early in 1919, and remarried in June that year to a lady with no obvious prior connection to him. Edith Naomi Wright was twelve years younger than Cecil, and when they married gave her address in Birmingham, where her father was working. Edith's mother had worked as a nurse in the past, and the family were originally from Peterborough. It is possible, therefore, that the family played a role in looking after Reginald during the war.

Kate Cunnington, for some reason, moved to Tunbridge Wells where she began a relationship with another Royal Engineer, Alfred Rostron, who happened to be married. In 1919, the law deemed that females could not divorce their husbands, but this changed with the Matrimonial Causes

Act of 1923, where a woman could divorce her husband on the grounds of adultery. Following Royal Assent of the Act, in the summer of 1923, Mary Ellen Rostron was one of the first to take advantage and submitted her petition for dissolution of her marriage on 10 September 1923, 'suing as a poor person'. She stated that 'from about the month of April 1919 to the month of September 1923 the said Alfred Cecil Rostron at 104 High Brooms Road, Tunbridge Wells, in the county of Kent lived and cohabited and habitually committed adultery with a woman named Kate Cunnington'. Both Kate and her late lover, Arthur, had now been named as co-respondents in separate divorce cases.

Cecil's life, after the turmoil of his childhood, the strain of life in the trenches, and the ignominy of his divorce, could finally start to return to normality. But not before a further tragedy, in 1920, when his newborn daughter did not survive. Cecil and Edith did not have any more children, but their marriage endured for over thirty years, until Edith's death in 1950. During this time, Cecil's career and standing within the communities in which he lived went from strength to strength.

In October 1925, Cecil moved to Belper as sub-postmaster and by the time he left, in 1932, he had become postmaster, president of the Belper Chamber of Commerce, and a warden at Christ Church. Cecil was presented with a pewter tea service when he left to take up his new position at Rushden, near Wellingborough, and was thanked especially for his consideration towards his staff. After Rushden, Cecil made his final move to become head postmaster at Frome where he lived, initially, on Marston Lane and named his house 'Rutland', a nod to his childhood in Exton. A few years later he and Edith moved to a more substantial three-storey stone house, 21 Locks Hill, which he named 'Rutland House'. Cecil's life in Frome, as in Belper, was centred around the post office, the local Chamber of Commerce and the church, where he probably sang in the choir as, in 1947, he was a founder member of the Frome and District Choral Union. Using his past connection with St John's Church, Cecil persuaded Sir Malcolm Sargent to become its patron, and the choir became well respected in the South West.

After Edith died in 1950, the sixty-seven-year-old Cecil was still active in the community and met Florence Hunt, a fifty-year-old spinster schoolteacher, who was also active in the church and a member of the Sunday School Institute. They were married in 1951, and lived together until Cecil died in 1967. It had been a long, and ultimately successful, journey from the Cheshire workhouse in 1886.

In 1919, Leonard Saunders, an engine fitter, moved into 7 Rock Terrace, together with his wife, Jessie, who remained at the house for almost fifty years (see profile 16).

PROFILE 16

A Link to the Present

Leonard Gifford Saunders　　　　7 Rock Terrace 1919–1946

Jessie Miriam Saunders née Smith　7 Rock Terrace 1919–1967

The Saunders family is the last link between a Rock Terrace tenant and a current owner of the same house. When the freehold of no. 7 was sold in 1967, Jessie Saunders was still living in the house that her husband, Leonard, first rented in 1919. At the time of the sale the layout of the property seems to have remained as it was built in 1842, save for the rear extension. There was no bathroom, and gas was the only means of lighting.

Leonard Saunders was born in 1896 in Manton, Rutland, and in 1901 his father was working as a railway signalman. The family lived at 7 Cornstall Buildings off St Leonard's Street, which had been built on the land that Richard Newcomb had set aside for his school that was never built. By 1911, Leonard was an apprentice engine fitter, and he went on to work as a fitter with a Stamford agricultural engineering company, possibly Blackstone's.

77. Leonard Saunders   78. Jessie Saunders

As no military records exist for Leonard it is possible that he was designated as working in a reserved occupation, especially as Blackstone's was manufacturing shell casings, and therefore exempt from conscription. In 1917, Leonard married Jessie Miriam Smith, whose father ran a provision's shop at 1 Castle Street (now 'The Kitchen' restaurant). A year later Doris, known as Peggy, was born, followed in 1923 by Irene.

Peggy, a keen swimmer, was, by the age of sixteen, an assistant instructor at the Scarborough Avenue Baths in Skegness and, in September 1934, she won the Town Challenge Cup in an open diving competition. Her youth and the ability to compete against local men led to suggestions that

Peggy was a future Olympian in the making. However, within six months, and aged seventeen, Peggy was married and did not defend her diving cup the following year, as she was pregnant.

Peggy's husband was a dairy farmer, and after their marriage they lived at West End Villas, off Foundry Road, and close to the rear of her parents' house in the terrace. Together they had four children. Years later, Peggy met the current owners of no. 7 at the rear gate of the house, and remarked that the yellow jasmine, which she remembered as a child, was still flourishing.

Irene also married a local man and together they had three daughters. After she moved away from Stamford, Irene maintained sporadic contact with the current owners of no. 7, and in a letter, written in 2001, she reminisced about the house that she and Peggy seemed to have enjoyed as children.

By 1939 both of Jessie's elderly parents had moved into the house, but within a few years both died. Leonard's death followed in 1946, leaving Jessie alone at the terrace. During the next twenty years she may have taken in the occasional lodger, but when the Potter family sold the freehold in 1965 Jessie moved, and lived for the rest of her life in Clare Close, another address off Foundry Road.

During this period women's rights remained scant, and both women and many men were disenfranchised, resulting in only one-third of the adult population having the vote. From 1903, activist members of the Women's Social and Political Union, called the suffragettes, led a campaign of civil disobedience to promote the right of women to vote. Many were gaoled and, in 1913, Emily Davison was killed by the King's horse at the Epsom Derby. Their campaign was voluntarily halted at the outbreak of war in 1914. The war, however, changed opinion and political will, and before it ended the coalition government passed the Representation of the People Act 1918, granting the vote to all men over twenty-one, and all women over thirty who met certain property qualifications.

CHAPTER 8

Tenants Preparing for WWII (1919–1941)

The First World War was over, but not forgotten, when in October 1919 Florence 'Zita' Todd-Newcomb decided to offload almost all of the properties that formed part of the Newcomb estate, some of which had been held by the family for almost a century. In retrospect, it was not the best time to sell property, but Zita could not have known that the market would bottom out shortly after. House prices had been in decline, as a multiple of earnings, since Newcomb built Rock Terrace in 1841. Then, house prices equated to almost fourteen times average earnings, and by 1911 this had fallen to a multiple of five. Three factors had influenced this decline: housing stock and average earnings had more than doubled during the same period, and

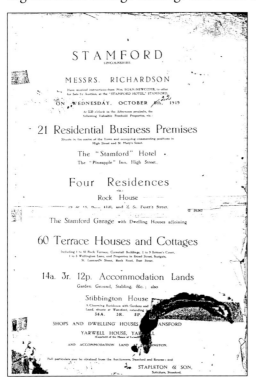

79. Richardson's 1919 sale catalogue

the houses being built were much smaller. Zita must have had her reasons for selling at this time, but in the event not all lots reached their reserve price, and those that did sell did not produce the sum that Zita might have expected. Included in the auction were: Richard Newcomb's personal residences, Rock House and Stibbington House; the Stamford Hotel; twenty-one residential building premises; and over sixty other houses and cottages. The auction was conducted by Messrs Richardson, descendants of James Richardson who had sold some of the properties to Richard Newcomb many years before, and who was for a time the letting agent for Rock Terrace. Richardson's had included all ten houses of Rock Terrace in the sale as a single lot, with the proviso that, if not sold in their entirety, each house would be sold separately.

At the auction, John Edward Cartwright Potter bought Rock Terrace, with sitting tenants, as a single lot for £2,500, and his family became the last landlords of the terrace as a whole. John was born in Dudley, Staffordshire, in 1863, and trained to be a printer. After 1881, he moved to Stamford, probably to work for Jenkinson's, the main printer in Stamford, and, in 1888, married the owner's daughter, Hannah. Three years later, John Jenkinson and his wife, Fanny, retired to 6 Tinwell Road, and John Potter and Hannah moved into the accommodation above the printing office at 58 High Street (now F Hinds, the jewellers).

80. 13 Barn Hill

When John Jenkinson died in 1898, Potter inherited the business through his wife, and changed the business name to J E C Potter. After years of living above the shop, the Potter family moved to 24 St Mary's Street, which they rented from the Newcomb estate, and which had previously been let to John Paradise. By the time Rock Terrace came to auction, Potter was living at The Nuns, a large property on the south-western edge of Stamford, which subsequently became a boarding house for Stamford High School for Girls. Besides Rock Terrace, Potter also bought 13 Barn Hill, (previously let to James Richardson) and as he remained at The Nuns, the two acquired lots were bought as investments.

Four years on from the end of WWI, families in Stamford continued to mourn their losses, and nationally there was little sign that victory would bring better times, although some attempts to restructure after the war were to prove a success. In particular, the Housing Act of 1919 began a trend that would see local authorities forced to provide adequate working-class housing. Other Acts followed, culminating in the 1930 Housing Act requiring local councils to clear all slum dwellings and re-house their occupants. In Stamford this was an acute problem because, prior to the Enclosure Act of 1871, court housing had burgeoned within the town to provide accommodation for the poor. Over sixty overcrowded and insanitary courts existed and now had to be torn down, to be replaced by new social housing. Whilst this was a positive move, initially, it was a slow process, and by 1922 little had changed in Stamford. What was evident in the town was the country's decline into recession. Unemployment rose and businesses in Stamford, including the Hayes carriage company, were forced to close or move to short-time working.

Margaret, the widow of Albert Hayes, moved back into Rock Terrace in 1923 and was one of twelve occupants at no. 10 during the eighteen years until 1941, giving rise to the assumption mentioned earlier that this property may have been reserved for short-term tenants. Elsewhere in the terrace, occupants remained a mix of widows, retirees and a few that were still working, and there was little sign that the country's turmoil had increased the turnover of tenants. In 1924, Elizabeth Grotten, the wife of a Russian merchant, and Harry Lenton, a retired shoe dealer died at nos. 3 and 5 respectively, and in the same year Stamford Corporation bought Hayes & Son's worksite on Scotgate in order to build a fire station.

In Europe the political landscape was changing as some countries ushered in new ultra-right-wing groups. In Italy, in 1919, Benito Mussolini founded the National Fascist Party, and in the same year Germany adopted a new constitution under the Weimar Republic. In 1921, as the hyperinflation of the Weimar Republic took hold, Adolf Hitler became Führer of the Nazi Party. With hindsight, these developments can be seen as a portent of what would follow.

British fascism, following Italy and Germany's lead, had been reported as a growing force in the local press, and at the end of 1924 something remarkable and unique in the UK occurred in Stamford's local elections. Arnold Leese was a respected local vet, living in upmarket St George's Square, but was also a fascist and rabid anti-Semite. He heavily promoted his views in Stamford and the surrounding villages. It was the British Fascist Party's view that its members should not participate in the UK's democratic system, but, in 1924, Leese and fellow member Harry Simpson, a local engineer, rowed against this view. Stamford Conservatives failed to put up any opposition against two Labour candidates, and Leese and Simpson were so appalled that they decided to contest the council seats themselves. To the surprise of the Stamford community, both succeeded and became the first Fascists to be democratically elected in the UK.

81. Arnold Lease

At that time, George Edward Potter, the eldest son of J E C Potter, who had bought Rock Terrace a few years before, was living at 4 Primrose Villas, Wothorpe. After leaving the army he worked as a commercial traveller, but it appears that alcohol was getting the better of him, possibly a sign of post-traumatic stress disorder, after spending almost two years on the front line in France with the 6th Lincolnshire Regiment. In 1925, he moved into 10 Rock Terrace, but in October he found himself remanded in custody at Oundle, having stolen two silver altar vases from All Saints' Church, Easton-on-the-Hill.

George's father, described as one of Stamford's most respected citizens, must have been embarrassed by the situation, especially as his son was refused bail, because, had he been released, he would have been re-arrested for other offences. Apparently, there were five other cases of theft from churches, and George had also been summonsed for dangerous driving in Leicester, where he had knocked over a policeman. His case was heard at Oundle petty sessions, chaired by Colonel Wickham, where George pleaded guilty. In his defence, the court was told that since the war he had become a wreck through drink, and his friend, neighbour, and fellow army officer Frederick Lenton stated that George had been a studious character. George's solicitor suggested to the court that if his client was placed on probation he would take himself off 'to the Colonies', where one assumes the aim was to facilitate some sort of recovery. The court accepted the suggestion; George was released, he moved out of Rock Terrace, and on 31 October sailed to Capetown. When he returned the following January, he gave an address in Brierley Hill, close to where his father's family came from, but little is known of his life thereafter.

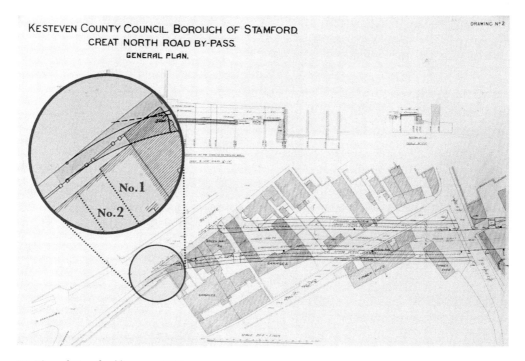

82. Plan of Stamford bypass, 1927

George Potter was not the only one with post-war issues. Some would suffer a similar fate, and others would be impacted by unemployment and political turmoil, which led to the General Strike of 1926. To help alleviate unemployment, a programme of public work was contemplated, as is now being mooted in the post-pandemic world of today. In Stamford, there had been calls for a bypass to relieve the traffic congestion from St Martin's, through Red Lion Square, and out to the Scotgate and North Road junction. This may have been one such public project, however, it was not a plan to bypass Stamford altogether, but one which would have scarred Stamford as we know it today, and impacted Rock Terrace. The proposed route would have run off of High Street, St Martin's, down Wothorpe Road, across the River Welland where the current footbridge stands, up St Peter's Hill, across St Peter's Street, through what is now Torkington Gardens, and across to Rock Road, where it would sweep down and join Scotgate. This act of urban vandalism would have required the compulsory purchase of fourteen cottages, two private residences, and four public houses, plus gardens and land. The Green Man Inn was to have been demolished, together with the now listed 30 and 31 Scotgate, and the pavement of the new road would have taken out the front gate piers of both 1 and 2 Rock Terrace. Luckily, the powers that be never seemed to settle on a forever-changing plan, and there were numerous objections that continued until WWII put the project on hold. The plan to cut through town was never resurrected, and its inhabitants had to wait until 1960 for the A1 dual-carriage bypass to alleviate the traffic problem.

Humphrey Burgess, the son of a stationer from Essex, moved to Stamford in the early 1920s, where he became secretary to Albert Cliff, thrice times mayor of Stamford and Chairman of Williamson Cliff, the brickmakers. In 1927, Cliff died and bequeathed Burgess four hundred £1 ordinary shares in the brick company. Humphrey became general manager of Williamson Cliff, and lived at 65 Scotgate (now Blo, the hairdressers) with his sister Joan, a nurse. In 1929, Humphrey married Elsie Thomas, the daughter of a wine and spirit merchant living and trading at 11 Broad Street. Unfortunately, in the same year, Joan Burgess died of acute leukaemia, and Humphrey, together with his new wife, moved into 1 Rock Terrace. In 1931, Humphrey's brother-in-law Leslie and his wife also moved into the terrace at no. 9, where they remained until 1933 when Leslie and Elsie's father died. Having inherited the wine business, Leslie, Humphrey and their families all moved out of the terrace and into 11 Broad Street, which would remain the location for wine and spirit businesses until a few years ago (now the Ghurka Oven restaurant). Humphrey later became one of forty-one employees of Williamson Cliff who joined up during WWII, but his story has never fully been told (see profile 19).

William Godfrey Phillips had been in situ at 4 Rock Terrace since 1922. He was a partner of Stapletons, the solicitors, and deputy coroner for Stamford and Rutland. He became coroner for Stamford in 1929, moved out of the terrace to 12 Tinwell

Road in 1938, and became coroner for South Kesteven in 1941.

By 1933, besides those mentioned above, there was an eclectic group of tenants at the terrace: Frederick Gooch, a vet; Charles Parsley, a baker and restaurant owner; Wilfred Foster, a farmer's son; Leonard Saunders, engine fitter; Charles Hall, superintendent of Stamford market; and Pierce Sullivan a steam laundry proprietor. Also present and living at no. 1 was sculptor Mahomet Phillips (see profile 18). Mahomet was of mixed race and would have been an unusual sight in and around Stamford, a town that even today is not known for its ethnic diversity.

PROFILE 18

Mr Phil, the Sculptor

Mahomet Thomas Phillips   1 Rock Terrace 1933–1943

Mahomet was born at Banana, in the lower Congo basin. His father, Richard Cobden Phillips, had travelled from Manchester to the Congo in 1868 to work for the trading company Hatton & Cookson. This was at a time when the area was under the control of local tribes, prior to King Leopold of Belgium claiming the territory, after which it became the Belgian Congo. Not long after arriving at the trading post in Banana, Richard met a local girl, Menina Barros, allegedly a Bantu princess. In 1872, their first child Sarah was born, followed by Paul, Mahomet in 1876, and finally Nene.

Richard remained in the Congo for sixteen years, becoming well versed in the customs of the indigenous population. He was a keen photographer and a couple of his plates of Henry Morton Stanley are with the National Archives. Stanley, of 'Dr Livingstone, I presume' fame, was on the last leg of his African adventure when, in 1877, he arrived at Cabinda and was entertained for several days by Richard at the trading post.

When Richard returned to the UK around 1884, he took Mahomet and his youngest daughter Nene with him. His other son, Paul, had died a few years before, and his eldest daughter Sarah decided to stay with her mother in the Congo. In 1891, Mahomet was living with his father in Manchester, but later moved to York where he worked as a sculptor, and continued to study drawing at the York School of Science and Art. It was there that Mahomet first met W P Horridge, head of wood carving at Bowman and Sons, Stamford.

Mahomet was born into a family where pushing the boundaries of normality, in that era, was common: a father who was prepared to work in tribal Africa; a cousin, E J Harrison, who travelled to Canada and interviewed Mark Twain, before working in Yokohama as a journalist for the *Japan Herald*; and an uncle, J S R Phillips, who became editor of the *Yorkshire Post,* and was a friend of Bram Stoker, who created and wrote *Dracula*. Mahomet himself was a remarkable man. The arts came naturally to him, but he was also a prodigious sportsman who, whilst in York, excelled in rowing, football, boxing and Ju-jitsu.

83. Mahomet Phillips, working on Edith Cavell memorial

Mahomet married Mary Ann Morley, in Ripon, in 1899 and they lived together in York, before moving to Tottenham, sometime before 1911. When WWI broke out, Mahomet joined the Royal Field Artillery, 281 Brigade, and after sailing to Le Havre in the autumn of 1915 saw action with the 56th Division in France and Belgium. Apart from home leave, it appears that Mahomet remained at the Western Front for the duration of the war. After being demobbed in 1920 he moved to Huntly Grove, Peterborough, then in 1924 to South Road, Helpston, before finally settling in Stamford, and moving into 1 Rock Terrace in 1933.

During the war years Mahomet had clearly not lost his skills as a stone sculptor and wood carver, as he was soon in demand, working on some prestigious projects. For a time he worked for J Thompson & Son in Peterborough, where he carved the Edith Cavell memorial for Peterborough cathedral. He may also have worked on his own account or have been sub-contracted out, as whilst living in Peterborough he worked on the 4 ft 6 in. King's Beasts, seventy-six of which sit on the pinnacles of St George's Chapel roof at Windsor Castle.

It is not clear when Mr Horridge first approached Mahomet to work for Bowman's, but from that time he worked continuously for them until his death, rising quickly to replace Horridge as 'Head of Sculpting'. Bowman's were inundated with work after WWI, and, because of their reputation for ecclesiastical work, were responsible for many war memorials across the country. Mahomet's skill was such that he was responsible for some of Bowman's greatest pieces, including the WWI memorial screen, inscribed, 'In Grateful Memory 1914-1918', at St Martin's Church, Stamford. His work can also be seen in most of Stamford's churches as well as in the cathedrals of Bradford, Chelmsford, and Lambeth, and in Grantham where he carved their war memorial.

84. WWI memorial screen, St Martin's Church

Away from work, music became a hobby, but it also involved wood. His undeniable skill enabled him to make a violin, viola, cello and double bass, and he taught himself to play them all, performing with the local orchestra at Stamford's regular Gilbert and Sullivan operas. Mr Phil, as he was known, was undoubtedly a talented all-rounder, but he was also a universally well-liked individual. It is unfortunate the he is not mentioned more often in the literature for his exceptional sculptures and carvings. He died at Rock Terrace after a short illness in 1943.

At the same time, in Germany, Adolf Hitler became Reich's Chancellor, and a year later appointed himself Führer, and started to re-arm, in violation of the Treaty of Versailles. This was causing consternation in the UK and, even though war would not be declared by the UK until 1939, signs of pre-war planning was apparent at Rock Terrace as early as 1935.

Ernest Sullock, who, as a pilot in 1919, had crashed in Hounslow, was now a Royal Air Force Officer reservist, and moved into 10 Rock Terrace in 1935, whilst based at RAF Wittering. During WWII, Ernest was promoted to Wing Commander, and, as a talented pianist, he composed 'Mother for Freedom', for the organ, which was broadcast on BBC Radio in 1944. Sullock was quickly followed by Pilot Officer Herbert Lazell moving into no. 6, and James Gunnell, RAF reservist, into no.10, in 1937, and Flying Officer Francis Ward into no. 6, in 1938.

Flight Lieutenant Hugh McCulloch moved into 3 Rock Terrace in 1938, and, like Sullock, was stationed at 11 Flight Training School at RAF Wittering. McCulloch had joined the Air Force in 1928 on a short service commission. In 1930, he was involved in a mid-air collision at 4,000 ft over Iraq. He survived, but two fellow servicemen died in the crash. In 1942, McCulloch became Commanding Officer of the Royal Naval air station at Addu Atoll in the Maldives, which was a refuelling and service station for long-range aircraft.

Also in 1938, Helen Pinder became Stamford's first female mayor. This was not as unusual as one might imagine, with almost twenty other female mayors preceding her in the UK, the first being the pioneering Elizabeth Garret Anderson who was mayor of Aldeburgh in 1908.

Later in 1938, 11 Flight Training School was relocated away from Wittering, and the site came under the control of 12 Fighter Command, where 213 Squadron became based. One of its flyers, Pilot Officer Brian van Mentz, took off from Wittering on 15 September in his Gloster Gauntlet bi-plane, the last of the RAF's open cockpit fighters. Due to its engine placement it had poor frontal visibility, and as he was flying over Stamford he hit a two-seater Magister training aircraft. Both aircraft were uncontrollable and, following RAF procedure, van Mentz and the two crew from the Magister bailed out and landed safely. The Magister crashed into the Meadows without casualties on the ground, but the Gauntlet fell into the garden of 7 Lancaster Road and its fuel tanks exploded, setting the house on fire. The policeman on the scene was initially unaware that Mary Russel had been hit, but her badly burnt and unrecognisable body was later recovered from underneath the wreckage. Van Mentz, who had testified at Russel's inquest, went on to become a fighter ace, flying Spitfires with 222 Squadron during the Battle of Britain. The iconic image of a pilot playing chess, whilst waiting to be scrambled, is in fact van Mentz at RAF Kirton-in-Lindsey. In 1940 he was presented with the Distinguished Flying Cross by the King, attended by Princess Elizabeth, after being credited with destroying six enemy aircraft, and possibly three more. Less than a year later, he was enjoying a few drinks with fellow airmen at the Ferry Inn at Horning when the pub was hit by three bombs. Twenty-one were killed, amongst them, Flight Lieutenant Brian van Menzt DFC, aged twenty-four.

85. Flight Lieutenant Brian van Mentz DFC

Once war was declared, more aircrew passed through Rock Terrace: Flying Officer William Dalton into no. 9, in 1939; RAF reservist Hardress Vallance to no. 10, in 1940; and RAF ex Chief Technical Officer, Arthur Jarvis OBE to no. 9, in 1941.

PROFILE 19

The Untold Tale of a Japanese POW

Humphrey George Burgess   1 Rock Terrace 1929–1932

In 2004, the Williamson Cliff factory on Little Casterton Road in Stamford was demolished. Amongst the rubble were the remnants of a memorial, to the forty-one employees who had fought in WWII, which had been bulldozed in an act of involuntary vandalism.

86. Williamson Cliff memorial, Stamford cemetery

Appalled by this loss, a retired couple, who had a relative named on one of the memorial bricks, searched the rubble for two months, and stored the discovered remains in their garage. Ten years later, with Heritage Lottery Funding, the memorial was rebuilt within Stamford's cemetery, and included the name of H G Burgess RAF.

By the outbreak of WWII, Humphrey had risen to become works manager at Williamson Cliff, and had moved from Rock Terrace to Broad Street. At the age of thirty-five, and because the brickworks provided protected employment, Humphrey did not immediately enlist. However, in April 1941, and having been in the Air Cadet Corps at school, he joined the RAF voluntary reserve. He was posted to RAF Castletown in Scotland a month later, was granted a commission as a Pilot Officer for the duration of hostilities, and assigned to the Administrative and Special Duties branch. Although not a flyer, Humphrey was assigned to support 232 Squadron.

In November 1941, his squadron was posted to the Middle East, but the air echelon was diverted to the Far East. Humphrey's ground echelon was reunited with the flyers in Sumatra at the beginning of February 1942, but, as the Japanese invaded, a further move south, to Java, was necessary. However, when the battle for Java was won by the Japanese, on 12 March, Humphrey became a prisoner-of-war (POW). It was the start of a hellish three-and-a-half-year struggle.

At the time of his capture in Java, Humphrey may have witnessed the beheading of several airmen by the Japanese – a warning to all not to contemplate any subversive activity – after which he was transferred to Batavia (present day Jakarta). In the following twelve months, Humphrey was moved from pillar to post, and during this time was promoted to Flying Officer. He would later become an important leader within the British POW contingent. Humphrey spent the latter six months in the notorious Victoria Gaol at Jesselton, where upwards of 1,000 prisoners were housed in a prison built for forty. The conditions were so bad that dysentery and malnutrition were killing the POWs, and in April 1943 the Japanese hierarchy ordered the camp to be closed, and the prisoners transferred to Sandakan by ship.

At Sandakan, where the men were to be employed to build an airfield, the conditions became even worse, and as the war continued the Japanese progressively withheld essential medicines to combat dysentery and malaria, and supplies of food. Around 1,800 Australian and 600 British POWs had been in the camp, but beriberi and malnutrition increased the death toll, and the majority of the POWs were ill. Allied forces began to bomb the airfield in September 1944 and by January 1945, once the airfield had become unusable, the Japanese decided to move 500 of the fittest prisoners to Ranau, a 155-mile, jungle trek away. Only 455 actually left, and whilst three-quarters made it to their final destination the appalling conditions, lack of food, and jungle illnesses quickly reduced their number.

In May 1945, the second group of 536 departed the Sandakan camp. They were spilt into groups of fifty, and Humphrey Burgess was in charge of Group Nine. These men were in a far worse condition than those who had made the first march, and an increasing number, who became unable to walk on, were shot. Only 183 of this group reached the Ranau camp, and, worse still, only six from the first march remained alive. The fate of the remaining POWs at Sandakan was resolved on 15 June. Those too ill to move would be left at the camp to die, and the other sixty-odd would form the third march to Ranau. None of these reached more than forty-two miles towards Ranau, either dying or being shot when they could walk no further. The total of 189 at Ranau was all that remained of the

2,400 that had been at Sandakan a year earlier.

By 1 July, the 189 had become 100 and by 28 July only 42 remained. The Japanese government surrendered on 15 August, but the Allied Forces did not reach the Ranau camp until 20 September, when they rounded up the Japanese remaining in the area. Captured documents, which are now at the National Archives at Kew, show that the Japanese had recorded Humphrey as dying from acute enteritis on 3 August 1945, and the same details appeared on the Commonwealth War Graves Commission (CWGC) site. It is also what Humphrey's wife, back in Stamford, would have been told. But that is neither the truth, nor the whole story.

Name	Date of Death	Cause of Death	Place of Death
Smith, Samuel James	1 Aug 45	Acute Enteritis	Ranau
Hoigson Roy	2 Aug 45	" "	"
Sands Albert	2 Aug 45	" "	"
Burgess Humphrey George	3 Aug 45	" "	"
McCandless Joseph Robert	11 Aug 45	" "	"
Chopping Geoffrey Newman	12 Aug 45	" "	"

87. Japanese record of death

Over thirty years ago, an Australian lady, Lynette Silver, started to research the history of Australians fighting in the Far East and discovered information about the Sandakan death marches. Her dogged approach involved pouring over Japanese records, talking to locals, and interviewing some of only six survivors (all Australian escapees). Her book *Sandakan: A conspiracy of silence*, detailing the records of all Australian and British POWs at Sandakan, was first published in 1998, but her efforts did not stop there. She continued to work to identify the individuals in unnamed graves and worked with the CWGC in London to correct previously published information. Lynette has, since 1996, successfully identified thirty-five such graves in the Labuan CWGC cemetery, whose named headstones have now replaced those with the single inscription 'Known unto God'. Amongst those was the grave of Humphrey Burgess, who had not in fact died on 3 August, but had been entered in Japanese records to cover up the orders from the Japanese hierarchy that no POWs should survive the war.

On 22 August 1945, seven days after the Japanese capitulation, surrender leaflets were dropped over Ranau, where fifteen prisoners remained alive. On 27 August, Captain Takakuwa, despite being aware that the war had ended, ordered the execution of ten of the POWs. The final five, including Burgess, were told, that afternoon, that they were to be interrogated at Ranau HQ, and were led off under the supervision of Sergeant Beppu. On the way they stopped, and were given permission to smoke and sit in the shade. Beppu then gave the order to shoot, and all five were executed, totally unaware that that was to be their fate.

At the subsequent war trials, Takakuwa was sentenced to be hanged for murder, and Beppu received a fifteen-year prison sentence, also for murder. Flying Officer Humphrey Burgess had survived to become one of the

last fifteen at Ranau, but was cruelly executed. However, thanks to the painstaking work of Lynette Silver, Humphrey now rests in a marked grave. and the CWGC website has since been amended.

88. Labuan War Cemetery

89. Grave of Humphrey Burgess

Amongst all of these servicemen, en route for active duty, was a businessman, Horace Gladstone Twilley (see profile 20) who moved into 5 Rock Terrace shortly before the outbreak of the war. His political and pacifist views had been forged at a young age, in his home town of Leicester, but the move to Stamford presaged a change, at least outwardly.

PROFILE 20

Pacifist to Pragmatist

Horace Gladstone Twilley   5 Rock Terrace 1938–1941

The Twilley family, in Leicester, were working class, pious and politically left-wing, and Horace, born in 1886, was the youngest of seven children. His father, when attending a Boer War peace rally in 1900, was hit on the head with a cane. He died four days later, which was probably coincidental as the cause of death was listed as heart failure, and from then Horace was raised by his mother and elder sisters. In 1911, his mother and sister Gertrude emigrated to Canada, where his sister became the renowned poet and suffragette, Gertrude Richardson.

By this time, Horace had become a socialist, and a member of the pacifist Independent Labour Party (ILP), whose first chairman had been Keir Hardie. He was also working as a yarn salesman – a business area in which he would remain for the rest of his life. At the outbreak of WWI, Horace supported the ILP position against conscription, and he became secretary of the Leicester branch of the No-Conscription Fellowship.

However, when the Military Service Act was passed in 1916, and conscription was introduced, Horace was faced with a decision. One of his brothers had signed up, but Horace refused and became a conscientious objector. It was not an easy decision, given the treatment of the 'conchies' by the public and the army, and made even worse because Horace was an absolutist: refusing orders and the wearing of a uniform. Horace was assigned to the 4th Northern Non-Combatant Corps, but because of his refusal to comply was soon before a military tribunal and sentenced to field punishment, which was effectively torture. Being force-marched around a parade ground, in irons, for two hours at a time during his month's incarceration may have injured him, but it did not break his resolve. As a result of further non-compliance he was sentenced four times to imprisonment, including spells in Leicester, Richmond Castle, Preston and Wormwood Scrubs prisons, amongst others.

90. Horace Twilley, in later life

After the war he married Ella Stevens, the daughter of a land surveyor, and his pacifist views did not change. He remained with the ILP, becoming chairman of the Leicester branch, until his resignation in 1932. Aside from his political life, he was an amateur actor of some note, as in his performance as Mr Throstle in *Berkeley Square*, set in the eighteenth century, he 'gave a finished performance, with just the right amount of precision and dandyism'. His passion for amateur dramatics did not diminish as, besides being an actor, he was editor of the magazine of the Leicester Dramatic Society, a producer of plays, a speaker on stage technique, and in the 1930s chairman of the Leicestershire Amateur Dramatic Federation.

In 1935, he moved to Peterborough and continued work as a travelling yarn salesman. The move away from his childhood home may have given him the opportunity to reinvent himself, and put some of his past behind him, although his amateur dramatics link to Leicester did continue for a while. It was in Peterborough that he developed an idea to make low-cost cotton gloves, the forerunner to what would develop into an international business. However, his home within the cathedral precinct was not ideal as a base for a business so he moved to a small shop in St Mary's Street, Stamford, with a small warehouse at the rear, and accommodation above. The business grew rapidly. By 1938 Twilley and his wife had moved to 5 Rock Terrace, and shortly after the H G Twilley Ltd business moved to a factory unit on West Street (now used as The Yard, a children's play area).

Twilley was a model employer who treated his staff well, and gave them cloth to make dresses in their preferred style, whilst maintaining a corporate grey. Flowers were placed around the factory, and by 1945 a garden had been developed at the rear, with a fishpond, pergolas and even a stage. Despite employing only fifty staff, Horace employed a full-time gardener to maintain the site, now the flattened and gravelled carpark for Westside gym.

91. West Street garden, c. 1945

The company was successful and provided female employment throughout the war. It is not known how strongly Horace maintained his pacifist views, but he must have been pragmatic and kept them to himself, for fear of alienating both customers and staff. After the war another sign of his possible reinvention was his involvement in public service. He became a local councillor, (Independent not Labour), member of the governing body of the Stamford Endowed Schools, vice-chairman of the Kesteven Drama committee, and president of the local Chamber of Trade.

After a few years at Rock Terrace he moved to 15 Rutland Terrace, where he could see his West Street factory from a rear bedroom window.

In the 1950s Horace sold the business and retired to 53 Gilbert Street, Cambridge. The new younger owners carried on where Horace had left off and H G Twilley Ltd became one of the largest and most successful yarn companies in the UK, and beyond.

In the 1980s, the business that Horace had founded began to suffer. Demand slowed, the company shed workforce, and also changed its name to 'Twilleys of Stamford'. In 1993, it went into receivership and the brand was bought by a Yorkshire company, Thomas B Ramsden. However, some yarns under the Twilleys brand remain available to this day.

The days of Rock Terrace providing single residences for those of independent means had waned by the end of the nineteenth century: by 1901 only four of the houses had live-in servants, and by the 1930s many of the houses were homes to more than one family. This situation accelerated during the Second World War, and as multiple occupancy was probably detrimental to the internal condition of the houses, some investment between tenants would have been required.

The details of Potter's will suggest that his son, George, was still alive at that time, but also that there had been no rapprochement between the two, as he was only bequeathed £100, the same amount left for each of Potter's grandchildren. The other two children, Leslie Cartwright Potter and Mabel Fanny Bullard, née Potter, inherited the largesse of his estate, including Rock Terrace. Together they took the decision to start to sell the freehold of each Rock Terrace house separately. The first house, 4 Rock Terrace, was sold in 1946, and it was not until the final sale of no. 2, in 1969, that all of the freeholds were in the hands of families other than the Newcombs or Potters.

As each house was bought, the new owners were able to rejuvenate their homes to suit their needs. In the process the houses lost their internal uniformity, and in some cases lost original features, but externally Rock Terrace has not changed from the building conceived by Richard Newcomb in 1841.

APPENDIX 1

Ownership of the *Stamford Mercury* by the extended Newcomb family 1797-1929

Richard Newcomb Sr became the owner of the *Mercury* in 1797 and it passed through a further six owners, of the extended Newcomb family, before being sold in 1929.

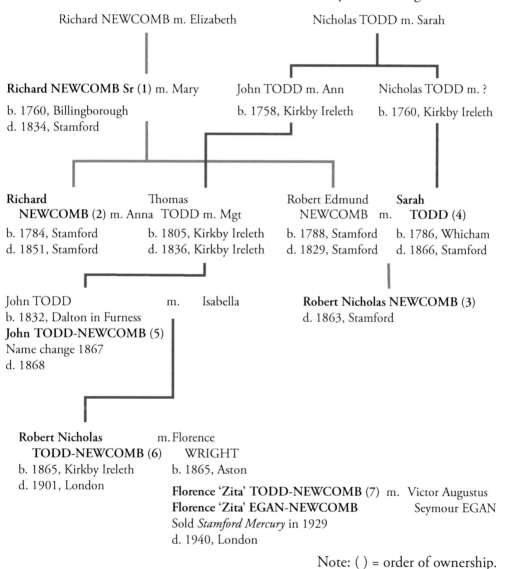

Note: ( ) = order of ownership.

APPENDIX 2

Newcomb's acquisition of land for Rock Terrace

As mentioned in Chapter 2, Richard Newcomb had not planned to develop Scotgate from the Green Man Inn to the junction with Empingham Road. Initially, he bought property for investment, and only when the last parcel of land became available did he contemplate rebuilding across a number of plots.

Richard Newcomb already owned investment property further towards town, including the Mason's Arms (26 Scotgate), and it is likely that he bought the Green Man Inn and its stables when it came to auction in 1833 for the same reasons (see Lot 3 in advertisement).

Newcomb would later use the stables of the Green Man Inn to build 30 and 31 Scotgate, and subsequently he or his heirs must have sold the inn, as it does not appear in the disposal of the Newcomb property portfolio in 1919. It is possible that Newcomb also acquired the small parcel of land adjacent to the Green Man stables when he acquired the Green Man (see Lots 1 and 2), however, it was certainly in his possession when he acquired the final plot.

Identifying the acquisition of the final plot was difficult. I was aware that Newcomb had leased land on Scotgate from Browne's Hospital in 1840, as local historian John Chandler had recorded this in his notes held at the Stamford Museum. His notes included a photograph of a plan of the land, drawn up by Browne's Hospital, and included in their lease book held at the Lincolnshire archives. Opposite is my

> Old-established PUBLIC-HOUSE and other ESTATES in STAMFORD.
> To be SOLD by AUCTION,
> By Mr. JAMES ADAMS,
> Upon the premises, on Monday the 6th day of January next, at 6 o'clock in the evening precisely, subject to such conditions of sale as will be then and there produced, unless previously disposed of by private contract, of which due notice will be given,
> THE following valuable FREEHOLD ESTATES: viz.
>   Lot 1. All those Two Messuages or Tenements, situate and being in *Scotgate* in STAMFORD, in the county of Lincoln, with the Yards, Shop, and Appurtenances to the same belonging, as the same are now in the respective occupations of John Barkworth and John Morris.
>   Lot 2. All those two other Messuages or Tenements, adjoining the last-described premises, with the Yards and Appurtenances to the same belonging, as the same are now in the respective tenures or occupations of William Eaglesfield and John Fitzjohn.
>   Lot 3. All that old-established and well-accustomed Public-house, called the GREEN MAN, with the Brewhouse, Barn, Stables (capable of accommodating 50 horses), Yard and Garden to the same adjoining and belonging, situate and being in Scotgate in Stamford aforesaid, now in the occupation of Wm. Wilkinson Bridges.
>   The purchaser of lot 3 will be required to take the Furniture, Stock in Trade, and Fixtures, at a fair valuation, and may have possession at Lady-day next.
>   For price by private contract, and further particulars, apply at my office.   T. H. JACKSON.
> *Stamford*, 19th December, 1833.

92. Adv. for auction, *Mercury* 20 December 1833

reproduction of the plan showing that Newcomb already owned land to the left of the plot.

Chandler, it seems, assumed that the land in question was situated on the right-hand side of Scotgate, walking away from Stamford town, and that the adjacent Newcomb property was Rock Cottage. However, plans such as this were not always drawn facing north, and this one did not have an indicator of the northern direction either.

Knipe's 1833 survey map of Stamford, which is very detailed and clearly shows Rock Cottage and the surrounding properties at that time, is drawn facing north. If the Knipe map is turned to match the Browne's plan direction, a striking similarity appears. It is clear that Knipe's survey matches the Browne's Hospital plan, with the wheelwright's barn in the bottom left corner. The Newcomb property referred to on the plan is, therefore, the land adjacent to the Green Man stables, and not Rock Cottage. The

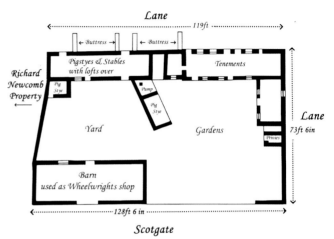

93. Reproduction of Browne's Hospital plan

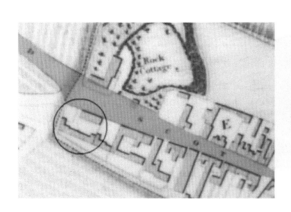

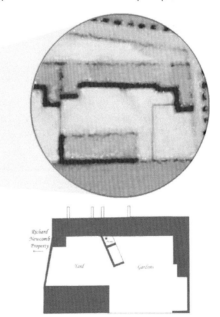

94. Identification of land on Knipe's 1833 map

lane to the right still exists, and the lane to the rear is now Rock Road.

Two further pieces of supporting evidence emerged. The first came from the *Mercury* advertisement for the auction of the Browne's Hospital lease, in 1840. It states that the plot was being used by H Hayes. This is Henry Hayes, the wheelwright, and provides a link to the wheelwright's barn.

The second piece of evidence is the location of the pump, marked by a square dot on the Browne's plan in the middle of the plot. This corresponds to a pump that existed underground in the garden between nos. 6 and 7 Rock Terrace. Because the gardens rose up from the house, to the higher Rock Road, Newcomb's contractor built an underground room, accessed by steps, which are clearly visible on the 1886 Ordnance Survey 1:500 Town Plan.

To be SOLD by AUCTION,
By Mr. JAMES RICHARDSON,
At the Woolpack Inn in Stamford, in the county of Lincoln, on Wednesday the 8th day of April next, at Six o'clock in the Evening, subject to such conditions of sale as will be then and there produced, either in the following lots or in such other as may be agreed upon at the time of sale,

Lot 1. ALL those 15 Acres of LAND, be the same more or less, lying dispersedly in the Open Fields of STAMFORD aforesaid, now in the tenure or occupation of William Spencer.

Lot 2. All those Eight Cottages or Tenements, with large Barn, Stable, Yards, and Premises, with Pump of excellent Water, situate in *Scotgate* in STAMFORD aforesaid, near to Rock Cottage, now in the tenure or occupation of H. Hayes and others.

The above estates are held under Lease from Brown's Hospital in Stamford for 21 years from Lady-day 1837, renewable every 7 years,

For further particulars, and to view the premises, apply to the Auctioneer, to Mr. John Roden jun., Stamford, or at our Office, THOMPSON and SON.
Stamford, March 26th, 1840.

95. Adv. for auction of lease, *Mercury* 27 March 1840

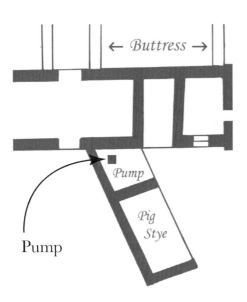

96. Location of Rock Terrace pump

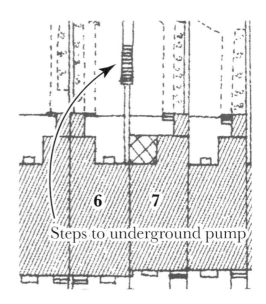

APPENDIX 3

Stamford Mercury employees in Newcomb properties

Richard Newcomb bought and held many properties in Stamford, primarily as an investment, and at one time the Newcomb heirs were reported to have had over three hundred tenants. This housing stock, including some of the most prestigious addresses in Stamford, provided homes for a number of *Mercury* employees, who would probably have made good tenants. There is no evidence to suggest that any of the properties were solely for *Mercury* staff, or that their rent was discounted because they were employees.

All properties mentioned in this appendix, both in the headings and the narrative, were owned by Richard Newcomb or his heirs. It is not an exhaustive list (except for Rock Terrace which is complete), but provides an indication of the many Newcomb properties which were let to *Mercury* employees.

Rock Terrace

John Paradise, Editor No. 1 (1845–1850)	Neither of the two larger central houses were available when Paradise moved to Stamford, but as his family grew, and he needed more space, he moved to 24 St Mary's Street.
George Dewse, Head Clerk No. 10 (1862–1864) No. 5 (1865–1872)	Dewse moved into an end-of-terrace house, as the two central houses were probably unavailable, but three years later he was able move to a larger middle house. In 1873, Dewse moved to 12 Barn Hill, where he remained until after 1891, having retired as head clerk around 1888.
John W Paradise, Reporter No. 9 (1868–1869)	This *Mercury* editor's son was, for a time, a resident at Rock Terrace. He gave up journalism, and in 1871 was living at 2 St Mary's Place.
William H Poole, Editor No. 6 (1894–1921)	After John Paradise died, William was appointed editor and was able to move directly into the larger no. 6, because Rebecca Southwell had died there in the year of his appointment. Rebecca was the mother-in-law of Edward Joyce (see below).

Clifford Joyce,
Publisher
No. 9 (1911–1921)
No. 6 (1922–1931)

Clifford started as a clerk, apparently became advertisement manager, before, in 1913, becoming publisher of the
Mercury. After William Poole died at no. 6 in 1921, Clifford was able to take his place, and, although he retired
shortly after, he remained there until 1931.

John T Scholes,
Publisher
No. 8 (1914–1926)

Remarkably, John Scholes not only spent his entire
working life with the *Mercury*, but almost all of his adult
life renting properties from the Newcomb family (Rock
Cottage, 31 Scotgate, 62 High Street as well as Rock Terrace). John started as a compositor in his teens, and rose to
become publisher in 1897, a position he relinquished in
1913, after which he retired to the terrace.

Brian S Ludlow
No. 2 (1924–1925)

Brian was a clerk at the *Mercury*.

2 St Peter's Street (Walsoken House)

Edward Joyce,
Manager
c. 1882–1923

Edward joined the *Mercury* as a clerk in the 1860s, was
its accountant by 1871, and in 1888, was appointed
assistant manager to Thomas Butler, the absentee manager representing Robert Nicholas Todd-Newcomb. He
moved into St Peter's Street around 1882, and in 1891
was listed as being the manager of the *Mercury*. Prior
to 1911, 2 St Peter's Street became known as Walsoken
House (after the birthplace of Edward's wife), and it was
as Walsoken House, with Edward as a sitting tenant, that
it was auctioned by the Newcomb family. The 1919 auction was unsuccessful, and it was not until after Edward
had retired in 1923, and moved away from Stamford in
1924, that the house was sold.

30 Scotgate	1901 Census	John Knight	Clerk
	1911 Census	John Knight	Clerk

12 Rock Road	1881 Census	John Bolland	Printer Compositor
		Harry Bolland	Printer Compositor Apprentice
	1911 Census	George Hibbitt	Compositor
13 Rock Road	1881 Census	Harry Pond	Clerk
	1911 Census	Henry W Pond	Printer Compositor
14 Rock Road	1901 Census	Walter Boyall	Printer Compositor

Cornstall Buildings

No. 2	1891 Census	William Bissell	Printer Compositor
No. 4	1881 Census	Charles Hodgett	Printer
No. 10	1881 Census	William Bissell	Printer Compositor
No. 11	1881 Census	John Martin	Compositor
No. 16	1881 Census	William Edlington	Printer Compositor
No. 16	1891 Census	William Edlington	Printer Compositor

APPENDIX 4

The Tenants, Visitors, Boarders, and Servants at Rock Terrace 1842–1941

The following pages tabulate the initial research to discover who lived at Rock Terrace, and forms the basis for this book.

Appendix 4a – The Tenants

This table contains the names of the lead tenants, or heads of the family at the property. Other direct family members living permanently at the house, e.g. spouses and children, are not listed. The entries are made to the nearest year, but with some caveats. Firstly, it is possible that preceding or following tenants lived at the same property in the same year. Where this is apparent a judgement had to be made in order to decide which tenant to allocate to a particular year. Secondly, some of the sources are directories for a specified year, and the cut-off date for inclusion in those directories is not always known. Finally, some sources contain errors: out of date information, incorrect spelling of names or incorrect initials or first names, hindering the identification of the individual.

Once the names had been collated, further research attempted to provide additional information, and where possible the entries include the name of the person, their date of birth and death, and their occupation or status. Where a tenant cannot be found for a particular year it is marked as 'available for rent' or 'tenant unidentified'. When marked as available, that information is usually corroborated by a letting advertisement.

Appendix 4b – The Visitors and Boarders

Visitors who are usually guests of the tenant are shown in blue and boarders/lodgers who are usually paying to stay in a property are shown in green.

Appendix 4c – The Servants

The servants have only been identified in the census years between 1851 and 1911. There are no servants listed in the 1939 Register. An attempt has been made to identify some of the servants who escaped this life through marriage or other occupations.

Sources for all sub-appendices:

Census:
1851–1911 and 1939 Register

Regional directories:
Whites, Kelly, Hagar, Slaters, Morris

Local Almanacks:
Jenkinson, Potter, Dolby

Electoral Rolls:
a few years, usually to check anomalies

Stamford Mercury:
Announcements for births, marriages and deaths
Advertisements for lettings and sale of furniture
Articles for council appointments, court cases, accidents etc.

	No. 1	No. 2	No. 3	No. 4	No. 5
1842	available to rent	Henry Jackson 1804-1874 Wine & Spirit Agent	available to rent	available to rent	available to rent
1843			George Pearce 1816-? Organist, St Michael's		Mrs Ann Anderson 1789-1876 Widow of Clergyman
1844					
1845	John Paradise 1811-1887 Editor, *Stamford Mercury*	Robert Secker 1809-1888 Gentleman			
1846					
1847		John Roden 1784-1849 Retd. Draper, JP, and Mayor	John Charles North details unknown Coal Merchant	Charles Walker 1819-1907 Draper	
1848					
1849					Miss Charlotte Twopenny 1791-1878 Daughter of Clergyman
1850		Joseph Thomas Wilson 1823-1874 Silversmith		Robert Michelson 1820-1902 Banker	
1851	available to rent		Mrs Mary Knight 1778-1863 Widow, mother of Richard Knight, Draper	available to rent	
1852					
1853					

No. 6	No. 7	No. 8	No. 9	No. 10	Year
available to rent	available to rent	available to rent	John Purvior Barratt 1815-1858 Singing Teacher		1842
available to rent	Charles Copping 1811-1868 Farmer	tenant unidentified	John Purvior Barratt 1815-1858 Singing Teacher	available to rent	1843
Miss Charlotte Twopenny 1791-1878 Daughter of Clergyman	Charles Copping 1811-1868 Farmer	tenant unidentified	John Purvior Barratt 1815-1858 Singing Teacher	available to rent	1844
Miss Charlotte Twopenny 1791-1878 Daughter of Clergyman	Rev Ellis Bowden Were 1810-1891 Rector, St Martin's	tenant unidentified	John Purvior Barratt 1815-1858 Singing Teacher	Mrs Sarah Newton 1791-1869 Widow of Schoolmaster	1845
Miss Charlotte Twopenny 1791-1878 Daughter of Clergyman	Rev Ellis Bowden Were 1810-1891 Rector, St Martin's	available to rent	John Purvior Barratt 1815-1858 Singing Teacher	Mrs Sarah Newton 1791-1869 Widow of Schoolmaster	1846
Mrs Sarah Coverley 1777-1848 Widow of Farmer	available to rent	John Rolt 1804-1871 Lawyer and Liberal Candidate	John Purvior Barratt 1815-1858 Singing Teacher	available to rent	1847
Mrs Sarah Coverley 1777-1848 Widow of Farmer	Rev Edmund May 1816-1893 Rector, St Georges	John Rolt 1804-1871 Lawyer and Liberal Candidate	Mrs Ann Jackson 1777-1849 Widow of Landowner	available to rent	1848
available to rent	Rev Edmund May 1816-1893 Rector, St Georges	Mrs Jane Smith 1778-1845 Widow of Draper	Mrs Ann Jackson 1777-1849 Widow of Landowner	Mrs Sarah Clapham 1814-1877 Widow of Surgeon	1849
available to rent	available to rent	Mrs Jane Smith 1778-1845 Widow of Draper	available to rent	Mrs Sarah Clapham 1814-1877 Widow of Surgeon	1850
Samuel Weddell 1820-1879 School Proprietor	tenant unidentified	Rev James Edwin Tunmer 1821-1919 Minister, United Reformed Church	Mrs Eliza Syson 1808-1889 Widow of Farmer	Mrs Sarah Clapham 1814-1877 Widow of Surgeon	1851
Samuel Weddell 1820-1879 School Proprietor	tenant unidentified	Rev James Edwin Tunmer 1821-1919 Minister, United Reformed Church	Mrs Eliza Syson 1808-1889 Widow of Farmer	available to rent	1852
Samuel Weddell 1820-1879 School Proprietor	tenant unidentified	Thomas Walker Blott 1823-1867 Commercial Traveller	John Charles Ridgway 1829-185 Music Teacher	available to rent	1853

	No. 1	No. 2	No. 3	No. 4	No. 5
1854	George Henry Chambers 1815-1872 Gentleman	Joseph Thomas Wilson 1823-1874 Silversmith			
1855					Miss Charlotte Twopenny 1791-1878 Daughter of Clergyman
1856	Samuel Fisher 1838-? Veterinary Surgeon			Mrs Elizabeth Priestley 1801-1901 Widow	
1857					
1858			Mrs Mary Knight 1778-1863 Widow, mother of Richard Knight, Draper		
1859	tenant unidentified				William Knight details unknown Coal Waggonner
1860		Garmston Chapman 1800-1872 Retd. Draper, JP, Alderman and Mayor			
1861					
1862	available to rent				available to rent
1863	Mrs Eliza Syson 1808-1889 Widow of Farmer			Joseph Bamford 1837-1901 Banker's Clerk	Robert Slagg 1831-1901 Draper
1864			tenant unidentified		
1865					George Dewse 1827-1903 Manager, *Stamford Mercury*
1866					

No. 6	No. 7	No. 8	No. 9	No. 10	
tenant unidentified	George Baker 1796-1879 Retd. Chemist	available to rent	John Charles Ridgway 1829-1859 Music Teacher	available to rent	1854
		Oliver Hunt Heazlewood 1793-1857 Retd. Surgeon			1855
				Thomas Alexander Greenfield 1829-1911 Bank Accountant	1856
					1857
Mrs Lucy Pepper 1794-1881 Widow of Farmer		Mrs Louise Heazlewood 1817-? Widow of Surgeon			1858
					1859
		Mrs Mary Pollard 1798-? Widow of Butcher	available to rent	available to rent	1860
			Mrs Martha Westrup 1803-? Widow of Miller	available to rent	1861
			available to rent	George Dewse 1827-1903 Manager, *Stamford Mercury*	1862
			James Henry Moore 1831-1904 Surveyor of Taxes		1863
					1864
				available to rent	1865
			available to rent		1866

	No. 1	No. 2	No. 3	No. 4	No. 5
1867			tenant unidentified		
1868					
1869		Garmston Chapman 1800-1872 Retd. Draper, JP, Alderman and Mayor		Joseph Bamford 1837-1901 Banker's Clerk	George Dewse 1827-1903 Manager, *Stamford Mercury*
1870					
1871			Henry Peake 1832-1900 Commercial Traveller		
1872	Mrs Eliza Syson 1808-1889 Widow of Farmer Mrs Eliza Syson 1808-1889 Widow of Farmer				
1873					tenant unidentified
1874					
1875			Miss Sarah Jane Guilding 1821-1879 Daughter of Clergyman	tenant unidentified	
1876		Mrs Elizabeth Kenrick 1805-1888 Widow of Solicitor			Thomas Dixon Beadman 1811-187 Retd. Farmer
1877				Richard Dean Holkings 1813-1892 Tailor and Hatter	
1878					
1879			Albert Henry Hayes 1846-1910 Coach Builder		John Foster Overbury 1845-1930 Editor, *Stamford Mercury*

No. 6	No. 7	No. 8	No. 9	No. 10	
			available to rent	Thomas Wingfield Hunt 1823-1868 Indian Civil Service	1867
		Mrs Mary Pollard 1798-? Widow of Butcher	John Worsley Paradise 1839-1900 Newspaper Reporter		1868
				available to rent	1869
			Charles Phillips 1803-1887 Lawyer	Rev Samuel Dodge 1841-1877 Wesleyan Minister	1870
					1871
Mrs Lucy Pepper 1794-1881 Widow of Farmer	George Baker 1796-1879 Retd. Chemist	Mrs Mary Hustwick 1810-1874 Widow of Clergyman	Jose A Gubian de Verdun 1822-? Merchant		1872
					1873
				John Foster Overbury 1845-1930 Sub-editor, *Stamford Mercury*	1874
		tenant unidentified	tenant unidentified		1875
					1876
					1877
		George Wingfield Hunt 1862-1912 Student of Holy Orders	Thomas Charity Halliday 1817-1884 Mason		1878
				Charles Marshall 1849-1891 Banker's Clerk	1879

	No. 1	No. 2	No. 3	No. 4	No. 5
1880					
1881					
1882			Albert Henry Hayes 1846-1910 Coach Builder		
1883					
1884	Mrs Eliza Syson 1808-1889 Widow of Farmer	Mrs Elizabeth Kenrick 1805-1888 Widow of Solicitor			
1885	Mrs Eliza Syson 1808-1889 Widow of Farmer				John Foster Overbury 1845-1930 Editor, *Stamford Mercury*
1886			T H George details unknown	Richard Dean Holkings 1813-1892 Tailor and Hatter	
1887					
1888					
1889		Buxton Martin Kenrick 1828-1889 Retd. Army captain	Mrs Jane Rogers 1826-1898 Widow of Haberdasher		
1890	available to rent	available to rent			
1891	Mrs Harriett Ellen Pollard 1830-1902 Widow of Butcher	Miss Elizabeth March 1853-1930 and Miss Caroline March 1857-1921 School Proprietors			Mrs Frances Skrimshire 1836-1915 Widow of Crown Agent IOM
1892					

No. 6	No. 7	No. 8	No. 9	No. 10	
				Charles Marshall 1849-1891 Banker's Clerk	1880
Mrs Lucy Pepper 1794-1881 Widow of Farmer	William Parker 1840-? Decorator	George Wingfield Hunt 1862-1912 Student of Holy Orders	Samuel Fancourt Halliday 1845-1922 Builder, JP and Mayor		1881
		available to rent			1882
George John Wightman 1853-1923 Ironmonger					1883
				Albert Bird 1848-1931 Coal Agent	1884
available to rent					1885
					1886
	John Enoch Mehew 1854-1904 Ironmonger	Miss Susannah Harris 1825-1901 Daughter of Farmer	Alfred John Taylor 1845-1893 Timber Merchant's Clerk		1887
				available to rent	1888
					1889
Mrs Rebecca Southwell 1820-1893 Widow of Solicitor's Clerk					1890
				John Thomas Brockliss 1854-1928 Chief Draughtsman	1891
					1892

	No. 1	No. 2	No. 3	No. 4	No. 5
1893				Miss Harriet Haystrat Holkings 1847-1934 Daughter of Tailor and Hatter	Mrs Frances Skrimshire 1836-1915 Widow of Crown Agent IOM
1894	Mrs Harriett Ellen Pollard 1830-1902 Widow of Butcher	Miss Elizabeth March 1853-1930 and Miss Caroline March 1857-1921 School Proprietors	Mrs Jane Rogers 1826-1898 Widow of Haberdasher		
1895					
1896				available to rent	
1897				John Enoch Mehew 1854-1904 Ironmonger	
1898		George H Brown details unknown			
1899		John Henry Thorpe 1870-1947 Ironmonger	available to rent	Alexander Bowman 1972-1915 Builder	John Hay 1834-1916 Retd. Farmer
1900					
1901				Edwin Ernest Pond 1872-1956 Solicitor's Clerk	
1902		Joseph William Bamford 1871-1932 Insurance Agent	Mrs Elizabeth Grotten 1838-1924 Widow of Russian Merchant		
1903	Miss Mary Helen Goodrich 1857-1928 Daughter of Coal Merchant			James Fuller Scholes 1834-1828 Retd. Cab Proprietor	
1904					
1905		available to rent			

	No. 6	No. 7	No. 8	No. 9	No. 10	
1893	Mrs Rebecca Southwell 1820-1893 Widow of Solicitor's Clerk	Mrs Mary Ann Sharpe 1819-1898 Widow of Farmer	Miss Susannah Harris 1825-1901 Daughter of Farmer	John Clarke 1862-1945 Horse Dealer	John Thomas Brockliss 1854-1928 Chief Draughtsman	1893
1894	William Henry Poole 1856-1921 Editor, *Stamford Mercury*				Mrs Susannah Young 1836-1926 Widow of Grocer	1894
1895						1895
1896						1896
1897					Rev Dan Wrigley 1870-1954 Curate, All Saint's	1897
1898						1898
1899		available to rent			available to rent	1899
1900		William Frederick Horton 1854-1915 Building Surveyor			John Coulson 1861-1942 Bricklayer	1900
1901			Albert Elijah Bassindale 1877-1954 Timber Merchant's Clerk			1901
1902		William Grimley 1866-? Retd. Engineer			John William Hilliam 1853-1911 Stonecarver	1902
1903						1903
1904		Alfred Herbert Coley 1879-1946 Piano Tuner	Mrs R W Moore details unknown			1904
1905					available to rent	1905

	No. 1	No. 2	No. 3	No. 4	No. 5
1906	Miss Mary Ellen Goodrich 1857-1928 Daughter of Coal Merchant	available to rent	Mrs Elizabeth Grotten 1838-1924 Widow of Russian Merchant	James Fuller Scholes 1834-1828 Retd. Cab Proprietor	John Hay 1834-1916 Retd. Farmer
1907					
1908		Mrs Minnie Ann Wright 1857-1942 Widow, Rate Collector, Baker and Mayor		Herbert Howard Small 1881-1958 Bank Clerk	William King 1854-? Retd. Manager, George Hotel
1909					
1910					
1911					available to rent
1912					
1913					
1914		Edwin Ernest Pond 1871-1956 Solicitors Clerk		Cecil Herbert Cunnington 1883-1967 GPO Telegraphist/ Sorting Clerk	
1915					
1916					Harry Samuel Lenton 1856-1924 Retd. Shoe Dealer
1917					
1918		available to rent		available to rent	

No. 6	No. 7	No. 8	No. 9	No. 10	
William Henry Poole 1856-1921 Editor, *Stamford Mercury*	Alfred Herbert Coley 1879-1946 Piano Tuner	available to rent	John Clarke 1862-1945 Horse Dealer	available to rent	1906
			available to rent	available to rent	1907
					1908
	Robert Sharpe 1872-? Bricklayer		John Surtees 1879-1911 Manager, Electricity Co.	John Taylor Sewell 1861-1918 Retd. Farmer	1909
	Earle Wedge 1855-1936 Engineer	George Murthwaite details unknown		available to rent	1910
				Thomas Harry Chesterfield 1878-1968 Grocer	1911
		available to rent		available to rent	1912
	Percy John Murrell 1884-1918 Organist and Music Teacher				1913
		John Thomas Scholes 1846-1928 Retd. Publisher *Stamford Mercury*	Clifford Joyce 1880-1931 Publisher, *Stamford Mercury*		1914
	Miss Mason details unknown			Mrs Sarah Jane Hilliam 1859-1948 Widow of Stonecarver	1915
					1916
	available to rent			available to rent	1917
					1918

	No. 1	No. 2	No. 3	No. 4	No. 5
1919		James Sydney Jones 1895-1955 Agricultural Engineer			
1920				Mrs Bertha C. Pearson 1873-1956 Widow of Carpenter	
1921	Miss Mary Ellen Goodrich 1857-1928 Daughter of Coal Merchant	Mrs Eunice Mary Dickinson 1864-1923 Widow of Chemist	Mrs Elizabeth Grotten 1838-1924 Widow of Russian Merchant		Harry Samuel Lenton 1856-1924 Retd. Shoe Dealer
1922					
1923					
1924		Brian Stanley Ludlow 1900-1947 Accountant and Merchant			
1925					
1926				William Godfrey Phillips 1884-1942 Solicitor & Dep. Coroner	
1927		Walter Frederick Hardy 1890-1982 Grocer's Assistant	Miss Fanny Burrows 1855-1942 Sister of Eliz.Grotten and Miss Constance Grotten 1865-1935 Daughter of Eliz. Grotten		Mrs Charlotte Lenton 1853-1931 Widow of Shoe Dealer
1928					
1929	Humphrey George Burgess 1904-1945 Works Manager Williamson, Cliff				
1930		Frederick W L Gooch 1898-1990 Veterinary Surgeon			
1931					

No. 6	No. 7	No. 8	No. 9	No. 10	
					1919
William Henry Poole 1856-1921 Editor, *Stamford Mercury*			Clifford Joyce 1880-1931 Publisher, *Stamford Mercury*	Percy Llewelyn Adams 1884-1971 Director, Lime Quarry	1920
					1921
		John Thomas Scholes 1846-1928 Retd. Publisher *Stamford Mercury*		Mrs Margaret Emma Hayes 1851-1930 Widow of Coach Builder	1922
					1923
				available to rent	1924
Clifford Joyce 1880-1931 Publisher, *Stamford Mercury*	Leonard Gifford Saunders 1896-1946 Engine Fitter		Frank Beardsall 1879-1928 Retd. Accountant	George Edward Potter 1889-? Son of J E C Potter	1925
				Cyril Frank Symonds 1895-1942 Fitter	1926
					1927
		Charles William Hall 1868-1935 Market Superintendant		Mrs Kate Ellen Owen 1881-1964 Widow of Shop Assistant	1928
			Mrs Jane Aughton 1867-1957 Widow of Parcel Office Mgr.		1929
			Leslie Thomas 1902-1982 Wine Merchant	Pierce William Sullivan 1889-1964 Steam Laundry Proprietor	1930
					1931

	No. 1	No. 2	No. 3	No. 4	No. 5
1932	Humphrey George Burgess 1904-1945 Works Manager	Frederick W L Gooch 1898-1990 Veterinary Surgeon	Miss Fanny Burrows 1855-1942 Sister of Eliz.Grotten and		Charles David Parsley 1894-1977 Baker & Restaurant Owner
1933					
1934		available to rent	Miss Constance Grotten 1865-1935 Daughter of Eliz. Grotten	William Godfrey Phillips 1884-1942 Solicitor & Dep. Coroner	Harry Garland Cooke 1897-1968 Civil Servant
1935	Mahomet Phillips 1876-1943 Sculptor	Samuel Bennett 1898-1980 Friendly Society Manager			
1936		Arthur Rowland Crowder 1891-1955 Friendly Society Manager	David Josiah Close details unknown		available to rent
1937			Hugh Lindsay McCulloch 1904-1975 Flight Lieutenant		
1938					
1939		John Edward Phillips 1898-1971 Service Engineer	Arthur Stephen Farrow 1896-1978 Engineer	Richard H Preston 1915-1993 Asphalt Layer	Horace Gladstone Twilley 1886-1961 Yarn Manufacturer
1940				Miss Blair details unknown	
1941					

No. 6	No. 7	No. 8	No. 9	No. 10	
Wilfred Kenneth Foster 1902-1965 Son of Farmer	Leonard Gifford Saunders 1896-1946 Engine Fitter	Charles William Hall 1868-1935 Market Superintendant	Leslie Thomas 1902-1982 Wine Merchant	Pierce William Sullivan 1889-1964 Steam Laundry Proprietor	1932
				Alfred John Bettle 1872-1959 Grocery Manager	1933
			Sydney Stannard Marjoram 1883-1963 Engine Turner	A H Drayton details unknown	1934
available to rent				Edward Arthur Sullock 1895-1968 RAF Reserve	1935
C W Barker details unknown Possibly RAF		Alfred Charles Dixon Hall 1901-1956 Motor Engineer		Percy Henry Clarke 1921-1943 RAF Reserve	1936
Herbert Lazelle Pilot Officer RAFR and Francis Henry Ward Flying Officer				James John Gunnell 1906-2001 RAF Reserve	1937
				available to rent	1938
William Ernest Dalton 1894-1946 Flying Officer					1939
				Hardress Constade Vallance 1896-1966 RAF Reserve	1940
			Arthur Nevill Jarvis OBE 1904-1954 RAF, Chief Tech. Officer		1941

	No. 1	No. 2	No. 3	No. 4	No. 5
1851 Census	unoccupied	Mrs Mary Webster b.1792 Mother in law			Mrs Ann Anderson 1789-1876 Widow of Clergyman
1861 Census	Alice Goodman b. 1837 Stamford Dressmaker				
1871 Census					
1881 Census		Rebecca Veal b.1796 Boston, Lincs. Companion / Mary Mercy b. ? London			
1891 Census	Mary E Goodrich b. 1856 Stamford Niece	unoccupied			
1901 Census	Mary E Goodrich b. 1856 Stamford Niece		Fanny Burrows b. 1858 Greatford Sister	unoccupied	Edith M Barford b. 1887 Grantham / James Edgar Jackson b. 1869 Tillingham Insurance Agent / Thomas E Halliday b. 1867 South Witham Builder's Clerk / Mary Ann Bradshaw b. 1877 Gt. Ravely Asst. in China Shop
1911 Census		Stanley Richards b. 1885, Tottenham Decorator / Basil Aloysius Ford b.1892 Selly Oak Bank Clerk	Fanny Burrows b. 1858 Greatford Sister	Marjorie Adine Palmer b. 1885 Clophill Dressmaker	unoccupied
1939 Register			Stanley G Simons b. 1890 Leicester Motor Engineer / Alexander G Willox b. 1894 Newcastle Foreman Electrician / George W Forsyth b. 1904 Sunderland Clerk of Works / Agnes Friedleben b.1874 Thornton Heath Private Means d. 1943		

No. 6	No. 7	No. 8	No. 9	No. 10	
	A Van Vloten b. c. 1827 Switzerland Teacher				1851 Census
				unoccupied	1861 Census
unoccupied					1871 Census
					1881 Census
					1891 Census
Henry E Bayman b. 1879, Peterborough Bank Clerk					1901 Census
					1911 Census
	Joseph Smith b. 1858 Carrington Grocer Father-in-law	Leonard P King b. 1916 Bury		unoccupied	1939 Register

	No. 1	No. 2	No. 3	No. 4	No. 5
1851 Census		Mary Page b. 1802 Swaffham Nurse / Elizabeth Crowson b. 1833 Helpston Domestic Servant	Mary Ann Fryer b. 1835 Swafield Domestic Servant became a Dressmaker	Mary Ann Hill b. 1830 Pilton Domestic Servant m.1853 Henry Baines	Jane Burrows b. 1811 Greatford Domestic Servant
1861 Census	Elizabeth Burdett b. 1832 Langham Domestic Servant m. 1861 John Hibbitt	Ann Coles b. 1840 Gt. Casterton Domestic Servant m. 1867 Wm. Crowson Wheelwright	Mary Chamberlain b. 1841 Oakham Domestic Servant m. 1873 Wm. Lattimore Bricklayer	Sarah Ann Clare b. 1842 Easton Domestic Servant m. 1868 Joseph Whinnett Carpenter	Elizabeth Watson b. 1840 Bourne, Lincs. Domestic Servant
1871 Census	Hannah Atkins b. 1858 Duddington Domestic Servant	Eliza King b. 1850 Stretton Domestic Servant d. 1871	Anne Grice b. 1855 Sewstern Domestic Servant m. 1885 Jabez Crofts Compositor	Sarah Thompson b. 1847 Wisbech Domestic Servant m. 1875 Frederick King Corn Porter	Sarah A Needhan b. 1856 Stretton Domestic Servant
1881 Census	Elizabeth Robinson b. 1860 Braunstone Domestic Servant	Mary Ann Hudson b. 1859 Sutton Domestic Servant	Mary Ann Hunt b. 1861 Pointon Domestic Servant	Jane Smith b. 1859 Grantham Domestic Servant	Emily Hill b. 1859 Easton Domestic Servant / Annie Littledyke b. 1863 Grantham Nurse
1891 Census	Kate Stanton b. 1873 London Domestic Servant			Mary A Rudkin b. 1872 Stamford Domestic Servant	
1901 Census		Louisa Bird b. 1879 Langrick Domestic Servant m. 1902 H Howell			Emma E Halford b. 1878 Ketton Domestic Servant m. 1901 Joseph Newell Signalman
1911 Census	Susan Russon b.1879 Stamford Domestic Servant				

No. 6	No. 7	No. 8	No. 9	No. 10	
Fanny Scoles b. 1830 Grimsthorpe Governess m. 1865 W Osbourne	Sarah Scott b. 1825 Collyweston Domestic Servant		Mary Atton b. 1834 Braunstone Domestic Servant		**1851** Census
Jane Fox b. 1811 Ireland Domestic Servant					
Eliza Fox b. 1835 Ireland Domestic Servant					
Sarah Burton b. 1822 Thorpe Cook	Elizabeth Crampton b. 1839 Toft Domestic Servant m. 1864 John Jenney	Charlotte Christian b. 1842 Uffington Domestic Servant d. 1864	Elizabeth Fisher b. 1843 Maxey Domestic Servant m. 1868 Henry Taylor Ag. Labourer		**1861** Census
Sarah A Woodward b. 1846 Helpstone Domestic Servant m. 1869 G Wood					
Phoebe Rhoades b. 1809 Stamford Cook d. 1898	Charlotte Laland b. 1852 Stamford Domestic Servant	Sarah A Blake b. 1850 Ketton Domestic Servant m. 1875 Geoge Porter Landlord PunchBowl 21 Scotgate	Emma Bore b. 1852 Stamford Domnestic Servant m. 1877 Arthur Coulson Carpenter	Rose Sharman b. 1853 Apethorpe Domestic Servant	**1871** Census
Susan Swan b. 1856 Ryhall Domestic Servant m. 1887 Rbt. Wakefield					
	Rachel Bacon b. 1853 Aby Domestic Servant m. 1891 J Beaumont Wheelwright	Eliza Greensmith b. 1858 Deeping Domestic Servant d. 1898	Harriet Burnham b. 1863 Stamford Domestic Servant	Kate Barton b. 1865 Stamford Domestic Servant	**1881** Census
	Louise Allen b. 1873 Barholm Domestic Servant m. 1896 Percy West	Sarah Alice Drury b. 1869 Careby Domestic Servant	Mary A Sharpe b. 1872 Kettering Domestic Servant	Emma Ringham b. 1868 Deeping Domestic Servant m. 1899 Samuel Rastall	**1891** Census
Alice A L Chapman b. 1873 Luffenham Domestic Servant m. 1902 John Eassom Baker				Minnie West b. 1882 Upwell Domestic Servant	**1901** Census
					1911 Census

SELECT BIBLIOGRAPHY

Adburgham, A., *Shops and Shopping 1800–1914*, London: George Allen & Unwin, 1964.

Bennett, W., *Absent-minded Beggars; Volunteers in the Boer War*, e-book, Barnsley: Leo Cooper, 1999.

Burton, G., *Chronology of Stamford*, Stamford: Edwards & Hughes; London: Robert Bagley, 1846.

Cooper, T., *Life of Thomas Cooper*, London: Hodder & Stoughton, 1872.

Davies, C., *Stamford Past*, Chichester: Phillimore & Co Ltd, 2002.

Davies, C., *Stamford in 50 Buildings*, Stroud: Amberley Publishing, 2017.

Drakard, J., *History of Stamford*, Stamford, 1822.

Flanders, J., *The Victorian House; Domestic Life from Childbirth to Death*, e-book, London: Harper Perennial, 2010.

Gilbert, J. L., *Wansford Paper Mills; Their History and Romance,* Wansford, 1974.

Hodgkinson, E. and Tebbutt, L., *Stamford in 1850*, Stamford: Dolby Brothers, 1954.

Holt, H. P., *The Mounted Police of Natal*, London: John Murray, 1913.

Jackson, M., *Chronology of Stamford 1840–1975*, unpublished, at *Stamford Mercury* archives.

Key, M., *A Century of Stamford Coachbuilding*, Stamford: Paul Watkins with the co-operation of Lincolnshire County Council: Stamford Museum, 1990.

Macdonald, F., *Victorian Servants; A Very Peculiar History*, e-book, Brighton: Book House, 2012

Markwick, W. F., *Stamford and the Great War,* Stamford: Dolby Bros., 1920

Nevinson, C., *History of Stamford*, Stamford: H. Johnson, 1879.

Newton, D., and Smith, M., *Stamford Mercury; Three Centuries of Newspaper Publishing*, Stamford: Shaun Tyas, 1999.

Pevsner, J., and Harris, J., *The Buildings of England; Lincolnshire*, Harmondsworth, Middlesex: Penguin Books, 1968.

Rogers, A., *The Book of Stamford*, Buckingham: Barracuda, 1983.

Rogers, A., (ed.) *The Making of Stamford*, [Leicester]: Leicester University Press, 1965.

Royal Commission on Historical Monuments, *Inventory of the Historical Monuments in the Town of Stamford*, London: H.M.S.O., 1977.

Silver, L.R., *Sandakan: a conspiracy of silence* (4th ed.), Binda: Sally Milner, 2011.

Smith, M., *Stamford Pubs and Breweries*, Stamford: Spiegl Press, 2006.

Smith, M., *The Story of Stamford*, Stamford: M. Smith, 1994.

Smith, M., *Stamford, Then and Now*, Stamford: Paul Watkins, 1992.

Stamford Mercury, 19th and 20th century editions, at *Stamford Mercury* archive.

Waterfield, A.J., *Annals of Stamford*, Stamford: 1887.

Yorke, T., *The Victorian House Explained*, e-book, Newbury: Countryside Books, 2005.

INDEX

As a local history book, focussed on Stamford, this index is biased towards its inhabitants and street names. All are included, even if only located in an appendix. Names are listed by surname in the main headings, except for the names of occupants, servants, and visitors of Rock Terrace, which appear under the Rock Terrace heading.